CREATING THE FUTURE

Perspectives on Educational Change

CREATING
THE FUTURE

Perspectives on Educational Change

Compiled and Edited by
DEE DICKINSON

ACCELERATED LEARNING SYSTEMS LTD.

Aston Clinton, Bucks. UK

ISBN 0-905553-32-2

First Edition

Mindscapes by Nancy Margulies

Typesetting by Anna Maria Blank and Richard Epps

Accelerated Learning Systems Ltd.
50 Aylesbury Road, Aston Clinton, Bucks UK
Tel.   (0296)   631177

Printed in the United States of America

To all who teach
It is they who create the future
for humanity

Acknowledgments

We would like to extend heartfelt thanks to the members of New Horizons for Learning's International Advisory Council, who have contributed so generously and insightfully to this collection of important thoughts about education. Their vision is already having a profound effect in guiding educational planning and practice today and for the future. And thanks to Nancy Margulies whose creative "mindscapes" connect and illustrate many of the important concepts presented.

Thanks as well to copy editor Dorothy Bestor and publications consultant Roz Pape, whose professional expertise has been indispensable to this project. And our gratitude to typist, Cheryl Senecal, whose flying fingers kept the project right on schedule.

To publisher Colin Rose, we extend our gratitude for making it possible to share these ideas throughout the world. We deeply appreciate his love of learning and dedication to improving the quality of education for all.

CONTENTS

Foreword

In recent years, Dee Dickinson increasingly has become both a catalyst for and an integrator of "cutting edge" ideas pertaining to the education of children and youths. "Cutting edge" may not be the most accurately descriptive word in that it conjures up for some people concepts that are new and perhaps untried. But the distinctive nature of Dee Dickinson's contribution is that the ideas she seeks to bring to the forefront are not necessarily new. Some have survived centuries of thought; most have a solid history in at least the 20th century. Clearly, many of the ideas synthesized are brought forward in fresh form only because they are sound and cannot readily be pushed aside. The irony is that many remain on the cutting edge, tried in only a few places, to disappear for a while, because they are overwhelmed by the relentless cycles of tradition and convention.

Another significant aspect of the synthesizing effected by Dee Dickinson is the extent to which she gives recognition to a wide range of relatively small projects—a school here, a cluster there, a school-university collaboration somewhere else, and so on. Hers is a celebration of grassroots educational reform. There is not anywhere in her work a movement or a "gee-whiz" advocacy of techniques designed for universal adoption. What is brought forward throughout is not a formula but rather sets of concepts and principles designed to enhance the largely self-directed learning of young people and the adults who work with them.

At the turn of the century, William James referred to "the soft and tender" and "the hard and tough" as characterizing the warp and woof of our society, and discussed the desirable tension between the two in the context of education and schooling. He saw these two elements combining in a strong fabric. Unfortunately, this is not the scenario that came to be played out in our schools or, for that matter, in education generally. Successive periods of reform have been strongly marked by either the hard and tough or the soft and tender but not both together. The excesses of one during a given period created the excesses of the other in a subsequent era. Reform, then, more often than not has been merely change rather than representative of steady progress.

The content of this book, *Creating the Future: Perspectives on Educational Change*, provide us with a rewarding example of concepts that, more often than not, appear to be somewhat on the side of the soft and tender. When one digs more deeply, however, it becomes increasingly apparent that educational principles and practices directed to the maximization of individual talent and potential are anything but soft in regard to their actual functioning, whether one is teacher or student or both. The setting of "tough" standards is easy. Holding individuals accountable for attaining them is easy, but also slippery. The true standards of individual growth are non-external, they lie within and can be met only by individual effort. The role of the teacher is to nurture this effort in every possible way.

There is only one disappointment in this collection of essays: each is short and one seems only to be beginning to enjoy it, when suddenly it ends. But to stop with this observation is to miss the point—the cumulative impact is enormous. Here we have the essence of the fundamental views of educational leaders who hold much in common, but whose particular perspectives and examples are unique. Just as Dee Dickinson in other work has introduced us to a wide variety of educational settings to commend, she introduces us here to carefully worked out ideas and proposals put forward by able people who have thought much about what lies behind their individual contributions.

In this period of thousands of educational reform reports, sweeping and often simplistic recommendations for educational reform, national slogans, and repetition of mostly the economically utilitarian role of education in our society, these essays are extraordinarily refreshing. I commend them to you.

John I. Goodlad
Professor of Education
Director, Center for Educational Renewal
University of Washington
March 1991

Introduction

Twenty-five points of view come together in this compilation of leading-edge ideas on education. Each writer offers a unique perspective based on a rich background of research or educational practice, and each contributes to "the big picture" that is forming of a new kind of education for our time. Considered together, their ideas are complementary; the sum total of these brief articles offers important implications for educational planning and practice. We draw some of these implications together in the conclusion.

Twenty-three of the writers are members of the International Advisory Board of New Horizons for Learning, an international education network. This network was formed ten years ago as a catalyst for bringing about positive change in education and as a resource and support system for educators seeking better ways of helping all their students to be successful at learning. The mission of the network is to "seek out, synthesize and disseminate relevant research supporting an expanded vision of education that increases awareness of human capabilities and offers educators and learners effective methods to develop these capacities more fully."

The new association of the Seattle-based New Horizons for Learning and the London-based Accelerated Learning Systems will move the work of *both* organizations forward into new dimensions. As one of the first joint publications, this collection of innovative ideas lays the foundation for a series on facilitating and enriching the learning process, and it harvests the work of many who have dedicated their lives to this endeavor.

During the last ten years, New Horizons for Learning has carried out its mission by providing current information to its members, publishing a newsletter, "On the Beam," and creating international conferences bringing together many of the experts whose articles are included in this book. These conferences have been the source of educational renewal for many schools, have resulted in new collaborations and projects, and have resulted in new networks of dedicated educators wherever they have been given.

One of the most recent conferences, "The Education Summit on Lifespan Learning" at George Mason University in Virginia, brought together experts in the field of education from pre-birth to old age. It was focused on the belief that intelligence can continue to develop throughout life, as long as, in the words of Marian Diamond, "individuals have an opportunity to learn in ways that are positive, nurturing, stimulating, and that encourage interaction and response." According to Diamond, who keynoted the conference, such learning and experience at any age creates better mental equipment and makes it possible to develop human capacities more fully than might otherwise be possible.

That is the hopeful theme of this little volume of bright ideas, which we trust will illuminate the thinking of teachers, school administrators, parents, legislators, business people, and other members of the community. There really is no limit to what is possible in human development when all the stakeholders in the educational enterprise share a common vision.

Jean Houston creates the context for the following thoughts about education by discussing the need for a new kind of education, followed by Arthur Costa's discussion of the need for a global perspective for educational planning and practice. Is it possible for a whole country to transform its educational system in the light of current needs and current possibilities? Luis Alberto Machado has proved that it could be done in Venezuela.

Reuven Feuerstein's Theory of Structural Cognitive Modifiability is the basis for understanding that everyone can learn—at every age and ability level. His work on the modifiability of intelligence is clearly related to Marian Diamond's research on the plasticity of the brain. Barbara Clark's development of an integrated educational program begins to put cognitive research and effective educational practice together.

Noboru Kobayashi's discussion of learning in early childhood underscores Paul MacLean's research describing the importance of the emotional context of learning. Jane Healy further describes what can happen when these views are not taken into consideration in planning early learning experiences.

The theories of David Perkins, Howard Gardner, and Robert Sternberg are complementary as they touch upon many aspects of intelligence and the importance of making it possible for people to learn and develop through their strengths. When that happens it is most likely that individuals will experience more frequently what

Mihaly Csikszentmihalyi refers to as "flow states," and that kind of motivation makes it possible for students to engage in transforming knowledge into the "deep learning" described by Noel Entwistle.

Cultural differences also account for the diversity in how people learn, as discussed by Asa Hilliard. Furthermore, as shown by Paul Messier, the uniqueness of each individual within a culture must have an opportunity to be expressed.

All of these ideas point to new ways of educating human beings, as Robert McClure demonstrates from his extensive experience in school restructuring. What happens when communities themselves become centers of learning? Malcolm Knowles dreams about that possibility.

As technology escalates, it is crucial to keep the human element in education. Charles Fowler describes what the arts can do to humanize the curriculum. In addition, Colin Rose points out how the arts can accelerate, deepen, and enrich learning, and how accelerative learning techniques have become essential equipment for teachers and learners in every setting. Linda Tsantis suggests that multi-media technology (a marriage of technology and the arts) can be utilized in ways that enhance the unique characteristics of each learner.

Lifelong learning becomes essential in today's world, as James Botkin points out in his discussion of learning in the workplace. The interest and involvement of the corporate community is now an important part of the educational scene. Learning goes on in every setting, but the environment is not always conducive to the process. Ann Taylor describes how well-planned architecture can actually become instrumental to education.

Shirley McCune presents a concluding piece on the process of restructuring education to meet the needs of diverse students and create a system where all can succeed. Clearly it is not an easy process, but she suggests ways to make it possible for any school.

Lest all these new/old ideas might at first seem rather abstract to teachers, we have asked Bruce Campbell, a third grade teacher, to describe how he has applied them to his own teaching. In addition, Linda MacRae Campbell, director of New Horizons for Learning and director of teacher certification at Antioch University Seattle, describes the processes of change that schools go through when they implement innovative methods.

The real value of publishing the current thinking of this distinguished group of individuals lies in what the reader will do with the information. We invite you to use this as a workbook. Write your reactions in the margins and open pages. Make notes of how you could apply what you have read to your work or personal life. Think of who else would find the information useful. Use the ideas as springboards for generating insights of your own.

The mindscapes created by Nancy Margulies illustrate some of the connections among the ideas presented. At the end of the book you will find a page that you can use to record your thoughts in a mindscape of your own.

Together, we can create a more hopeful future for students of every age, and for the students in coming generations.

Dee Dickinson

CREATING THE FUTURE

Perspectives on Educational Change

Jean Houston

Whole systems are changing. Every social institution is undergoing radical shifts, and educational systems must prepare our youth for a very different kind of world. No one speaks more eloquently of the needs and possibilities for fuller development of human capacities than Dr. Jean Houston, co-director of the Foundation for Mind Research in New York.

She believes that "when one is allowed to think and learn in images as well as through kinesthetic and other sensory frames of being, the world and its problems appear very different from the way they do to a more contained mindstyle. The total human then meets the total world, and the world and humanity are richer for it. It is inevitable perhaps that education will re-weave itself, toward this end, a curriculum that conspires to evoke the once and future human."

Dr. Houston is internationally known as a researcher and consultant on human development, traveling as much as a quarter-million miles a year throughout the world. Her intensive, high-energy workshops are imaginative and artfully choreographed experiences, blending myth, history, philosophy, and psychology with all the arts.

A philosopher and cultural historian, Dr. Houston has taught philosophy, psychology, and religion at Columbia University, Hunter College, the New School for Social Research, Marymount College, and the University of California. In 1985 she was elected Distinguished Educator of the Year by the National Teacher-Educator Association.

The following article is the only one not written for this collection. It appeared in Jean Houston's journal *Dromenon* about the same time that New Horizons for Learning was founded and was later reprinted in *Lifeforce*. An inspiration then, it is now even more relevant to today's needs for educational change. It is reprinted here with the permission of the author.

EDUCATING THE POSSIBLE HUMAN   Jean Houston, Ph.D.

Restoration of the child and through the child, the planet, is not only possible to us within the framework of our present knowledge, but is highly practical. With the enhancement of sensory and perceptual knowledge, with the recovery of imaginal and symbolic structures, the child learns the virtuoso capacities of brain and body and his mind grows in kind. Ironically, conceptualization in its finest forms is grounded in a refinement of perceptualization. In our research we find quite simply that there is a real equation between the ability to entertain and sustain complex thinking processes and the richness of the person's sensory and kinesthetic awareness.

In the dozens of cases that we have explored of high actualizing intelligence, of people who use their intelligence for creative accomplishment, the great majority of them we have found were stimulated as children with rich sensory and arts-related experiences.

Perhaps the most intelligent and sensitive person I have ever known also had the greatest subtlety of sensory refinement. Her name was Margaret Mead and she was far richer and more interesting than the person represented by her public image, remarkable as that was. She thought more, felt more, gave more, and got more out of life than virtually anyone I had ever met. In knowing Margaret Mead, I was experiencing a new style of human being, a new way of being human.

With her cooperation, I eventually began a formal study of Margaret Mead, especially of her thinking and perceptual processes. This study, which lasted five years, until her death in 1978, is especially germane to our consideration of the education and preparation of the possible human. Her early years particularly tell us much about the important effects of sensory and aesthetic styles of learning on cognitive development.

She was born in Philadelphia in 1901 into a family of educators. Her father, Edward Mead, was a brilliant, rather eccentric economist and professor. Her mother, Emily Fogg Mead, was a sociologist much involved in causes and community projects. Her grandmother, Martha Ramsay Mead—one of the principal influences in her life— was a strong-minded, innovative schoolteacher. After kindergarten, Margaret was periodically educated at home because her family had thought so much about education that they disapproved of formal schooling. Her mother gave her poetry to memorize; her grandmother dispensed hardy maxims for her to take to heart while her hair was being brushed. She learned basketry, carpentry, weaving, wood carving, and other manual skills requiring fine eye-to-muscle coordination (in which she surpassed nearly everyone else we have tested).

4

Following a suggestion of William James, her mother exposed her to numerous sensory stimuli when she was still an infant—colors, textures, pictures of great works of art, and masterpieces of music, including an ancient Greek hymn to Apollo retained in the Byzantine church. She was encouraged to use all her senses in any kind of activity, even the most abstract ones. Dualisms were discouraged; she was trained to accept the unity of mind and body, thinking and feeling. If you ask Western people where "I" exists, many point to their foreheads. If you asked Margaret Mead that question, she responded matter-of-factly, "Why, all over me, of course."

Of course.

Given this base of rich sensibility, Margaret acquired an unusual ability to store memories and learn abstract material rapidly. When a sensorium is as consciously developed to the extent that it was in young Margaret, then the child and the adult she becomes has more conscious use of proprioceptors, more "hooks and eyes" as it were, to catch and keep the incoming information, and then relate it to other information stored in the sensorium. Nor was she limited to five senses. Throughout her life she kept up her childhood capacity for synesthesia (cross-sensing) which most children have by then lost because it is discouraged. A synesthete can hear color and see sound, taste time and touch aromas.

Here is a classic exchange with a natural synesthete:

Me: Margaret, what does this room taste like?
Margaret: Something in which spices were put last week.
Me: What do you hear in Bob's face?
Margaret: I guess . . . a symphony.
Me: What is the touch of my voice?
Margaret: Your voice is a brush. It's a brush that's made of very
non-bristling material, so it isn't like a brush made of pig's

bristles, but it isn't as soft as the kind of silk brush that you use to do a baby's hair. It's somewhere in between.
Me: Not nylon, I hope!
Margaret: No, not nylon! It's something live.

Her kinesthetic sense was also developed early and sustained throughout her life so that as an anthropologist, she had the physical empathy to understand, through body sensing, the special skills of primitive cultures.

She could feel a complex fishing procedure in her bones and sinews, sense an intricate dance as a kinesthetic rhythm in her muscle fibers. Photographs of her in the field reveal her assuming some of the sensibility of the cultures she is observing. She appears soft in Arapesh, tense in Manus, unfocused and "away" in Bali.

Grandmother Mead insisted that she learn how to do entire procedures from beginning to end, so she learned not only how to weave, but also how to build a loom. Throughout her life whenever she began or joined a project, she invariably followed it through to its natural conclusion (which made for an extraordinary number of projects in progress at any given time).

In contrast, other people often dilute their actions and decision by employing what I call "the switch." To throw the switch is to modify one's world radically. The world becomes not weather, wind, and trees; not looms, threads, and chisels, but a macroartifact set in motion by an arbitrary throwing of the switch.

A gap of ignorance lies between the operated switch and the operating world. One is not only ignorant of the process contained in the gap; one is also removed several times from the environment that the machine operates upon. One becomes observer with little or no social responsibility, no sense of the need to follow through the organic sequencing of a process. One is the ignorant slave of abstraction, blind to process, a mechanic with little knowledge of his material, and even less sense of its possibilities. One doesn't know how to guide the beginnings, middles, and ends of things.

Grandmother Mead didn't care for drill, believing that it inhibited originality and spontaneity in children. If something was to be learned, it had to be learned right away, a skill Margaret retained all her life. In Margaret's experience, this involved employing more senses and ways of knowing in the learning situation. When she learned a poem, for example, she would join simple rote memorization to an inner process in which she actually saw the images described in the poem, felt the situation or event as vividly as if she had been there, experienced the textures and tone of the poem, and took its emotions for her own. As an experiment, the reader might apply these techniques in learning the following ditty in the same way the four-year-old Margaret Mead learned it:

> *I'm sitting alone by the fire*
> *Dressed just as I came from the dance.*
> *In a gown, Frog, even you would admire -*
> *It cost a cool thousand in France.*
> *I'm bediamonded out of all reason,*
> *My hair is done up in a queue,*
> *In short, sir, the belle of the season*
> *Is wasting an hour on you.*

In our own research with "problem learners," we have developed techniques quite similar to Margaret's multi-perceptual learning. The child is taught to think in images as well as in words, to learn spelling or even arithmetic in rhythmic patterns, to think with his whole body—in short, to learn school basics from a much larger spectrum of sensory and cognitive possibilities.

Thus, if children show inadequacy in one form of learning— say verbal skills—we direct them to another form, such as sensory-motor skills, in which they may show a greater facility to learn to read and write faster and with greater depth and appreciation.

Some years ago, while developing new teaching methods for what was bureaucratically referred to as "minority group slow learners," I asked an eight-year-old boy, "Tommy, how much is this: five plus three plus two?" Tommy made a face indicating boredom. I then upended the chair I was sitting on and began to drum on it asking, "Tommy, how much is this: bump bump bump bump bump—bump bump bump—bump bump?" Tommy grinned and said, "That's ten, man." "Why didn't you tell me before?" I asked. " Cause you didn't ask me before," he replied.

He was right. Most of our questions and answers in the schoolroom are addressed to one very small section of the brain, and arise out of one very small section of the planet: northern Europe. Much in northern European derived education and understanding of intelligence tends to reward those students who respond well to verbal, linear styles of education. And yet we humans are as different as snowflakes, one from the other. Our brains are as different from each other as are our fingerprints, with enormous variations in styles and talents of perception and learning.

Some people are naturally kinesthetic thinkers, others think in images, others in sounds. Classical education tends to inhibit these and frequently causes these nonverbal thinkers to feel inferior and begin a process of failure that will last all of their lives.

From many years of observation I have found that I have rarely met a stupid child, but I have met many stupid and debilitating, and yes, even brain-damaging systems of education. As we subsequently discovered, a child can learn math as a rhythmic dance and learn it well (the places of rhythm in the brain being adjacent to the places of order). Children can learn almost anything and pass standard tests if they are dancing, tasting, touching, hearing, seeing, and feeling information. They can delight in doing so because they are using much more of the mind-brain-body system than conventional teaching generally permits.

8

So much of the failure in school comes directly out of boredom, which itself comes directly out of the larger failure to stimulate all those areas in the brain which could give so many more ways of responding to this world.

Adding to this problem is our tendency to classify a person as either an artist or a practical type; either a feeling-sensing type or an abstract intellectual; either this or that - but rarely maybe. The message of the bilateral brain is that we are Both/And plus much much more. In today's complex reality we need to have access to all our parts. We can no longer afford to shortchange our brains and impoverish our spirits. Those limitations have now become desecrations of our humanity, the fullness of which is needed in ways in which it never was before.

Arthur Costa

Dr. Arthur Costa has done a great deal of thinking about "school as home for the mind." His insightful and compelling presentations to groups of educators move many to action in creating classrooms that are thoughtful places to learn. His words have been heard and read throughout the world. Indeed he is actively concerned that there must be world-wide change in educational systems if they are to meet the needs of a global society.

Dr. Costa is a professor of Education at California State University, Sacramento. He has served there as Chair of the Department of Educational Administration and currently teaches graduate courses to teachers and administrators in curriculum, supervision, and the improvement of instruction.

He is the author of *The Enabling Behaviors, Teaching for Intelligent Behaviors*, and *Supervision for Intelligent Teaching*, and he edited the widely used text *Developing Minds: A Resource Book for Teaching Thinking*. He is co-author of *Techniques for Teaching Thinking*, as well as numerous other articles and publications on supervision, teaching strategies, and thinking skills.

Dr. Costa has made presentations and conducted workshops for educators throughout the United States and in Canada, Europe, Africa, the Middle East, Asia, and the South Pacific. He taught in the Bellflower School District of Los Angeles, worked as a curriculum Consultant in the Los Angeles County Superintendent of Schools' Office, and served as Director of Educational Programs for the National Aeronautics and Space Administration for the western states.

Active in many professional organizations, Dr. Costa served as President of the Association for Supervision and Curriculum Development in 1988-89, and has also served as President of the California ASCD.

EDUCATING THE GLOBAL INTELLECT   Arthur L. Costa, Ed.D.

In this, the last decade of the century, we are witnessing a universal revolution of the mind. As a result of instantaneous global communications, entire nations have become increasingly aware of other societies' artistic, technological, social, and economic progress. Comparing other nations' prosperity with their own dismal existence has demonstrated to the peoples of underdeveloped nations the compelling effects of the applied intellect: creativity, problem solving, and reasoning skills in a climate of entre-preneurship, freedom, and collaboration.

As a result, entire nations are renouncing their brief experiment with intellectual depression. They have embarked on a revolutionary demand for the installation of those cultural, societal, and environmental conditions that promote the fullest development of the intellect: by greater involvement in creative problem-solving, democratic decision-making, and responsive interaction among the masses rather than decisions made by an elite few.

The human quest for intellectual fulfillment has never been more pronounced. Luis Alberto Machado's notion of each individual's inherent right to have his or her intellect developed is now seen manifest as a universal aim from South Africa to the Kremlin, from the Brandenburg Gate to Tiananmen Square.

Based on the two truisms that schools are a reflection of society and that modern society is becoming an increasingly global one, there is a quiet revolution taking place in education as well—a revolution of the mind. The restructured schools and effective classrooms based on collaborative learning, participative decision-making, strategic teaching and peer coaching are having a secondary effect: that of the quest for the intellectual empowerment and fulfillment of the individual.

I strongly believe that this global quest for intellectual empowerment and the more microcosmic but concurrent educational pursuit of participative decision-making are not merely coincidental. The parallel patterns are far too obvious. Both school leaders and national leaders are heading toward a new state of mind—a new perception of their role and that of their organization; from seeking power to empowering others; from controlling people to enabling them to be creative.

Surprisingly, perhaps, this is not so innovative an idea. The Greeks had a similar societal concept—Paideia—a society in which learning, fulfillment, and becoming human are the primary goals and *all* its institutions are directed toward that end. The Athenians designed their society to bring all its members to the fullest development of their highest powers. They were educated by their culture—by Paideia. Self-development and the promotion of life-long learning is the "central project" of society.

Jean Houston's remark, "Never has the vision of what human beings can be been more remarkable," takes on even greater meaning as we more clearly envision, more stridently demand, and more eagerly install those societal and noticeably similar educational conditions in which humanness is enhanced.

We are on the verge of a new century and the threshold of a new millennium. The young people in our schools today are the statespeople, leaders, parents, and teachers of the 21st century. Invested in them is our legacy: the idea of a world in the future in which humans can live in harmony with each other and with their environment.

The cooperative skills they learn in schools today equip them with the empathy to build the global community of the next generation. The problem-solving skills they learn in school today provide them with the stamina to tackle the immense problems facing our ecological future. The communication skills they learn today furnish the ability to work in the emerging corporate world era. Learning how to learn today fosters the continuance of learning throughout a lifetime. The fullest development of the intellect today makes it possible for them to continue developing visions of ever more remarkable human beings. The best way to predict the future, however, is to invent it now.

If our schools fail, then our society and the greater global society will fail. Whatever it costs, the price of failure will be greater than the price of education. Our children are worth it. Our planet is worth it.

Luis Alberto Machado

In 1979, Dr. Luis Alberto Machado, first Minister for the Development of Intelligence in Venezuela, and indeed the first such Minister in the whole world, began a project to raise the intelligence of the entire population of his country. For five years under his leadership there flourished one of the boldest experiments in education ever undertaken. With almost no budget, yet making the fullest use of existing institutions, the program was aimed at bringing about the fullest possible development of human beings in mind, body, and spirit.

Built on an eclectic gathering of the finest thinking of researchers from many parts of the world, the Venezuelan Intelligence Project was implemented through community resource centers for parent, school, higher education, and adult education systems, and it made use of all the media—publications, radio, television—to make the tools of thinking available to all. During the ten years since the inception of the project, new technology has become available to be utilized in ways Dr. Machado could only dream of at the time. The project stands as a model waiting to be replicated.

Dr. Machado has spent most of his life in academic and public positions in Venezuela. He has written a number of books on philosophy and social science, including the widely acclaimed *La Revolucion de la Inteligencia.* His more recent book, *The Right to be Intelligent,* a translation of *El Derecho a ser Inteligente,* reads like an epic poem for our time. In it he argues that there are no genetic determinants of intelligence and that only education can produce change. He writes, "No one is born civilized or primitive... The difference between a primitive man and a civilized one is not biological; it is educational."

UNIVERSAL GOAL   Luis Alberto Machado, Ph.D.

Every man has the natural right to develop his own genetic potentiality and the right to use all the existing scientific knowledge that can facilitate this development. Therefore society has the duty to make the fruits of science available to all people. In the fulfillment of this duty, and as a proof of his will to make education the priority task of his Government, the President of Venezuela, Luis Herrera Campins, at the beginning of his Administration in March 1979, appointed a Minister of State for the Development of Intelligence.

With this decision, a president for the first time in history granted a political dimension to intelligence and its development.

15

The goal was that intelligence become a fruitful reality in the hands of the majority, and not the unique attribute of a few privileged individuals. It involves the democratization of science. This means that all scientific knowledge that can contribute to the development of the genetic capacity of human beings—the most valuable inheritance man can have—be used by them all.

The development of the intelligence of all people has to be the fundamental aim of our times. To guarantee peace, democracy, and freedom throughout the world, the development of the intelligence of each and every citizen has to become a national goal in all countries of the world: a universal goal.

Violence under any of its forms will always be a manifestation of barbarism: among animals, the only law. Nothing is gained with war, terrorism, threats. Everything is to be gained with peace. Through the development of the people's intelligence, some day there will be no more violence in the world.

Democracy is the result of the will and intelligence of people. To make democracy possible we need a "democratic person"—a man who does not only fervently desire democracy, but who can also generate within himself the faculties needed to live democracy. If democracy is the government of the people, the people's capacity for participation must grow continuously.

The democratization of science is a basic requirement for a true democracy in which everyone can receive the benefits of science, accomplishing at the same time an active role in the country's developmental process and in the determination of his or her own destiny.

The development of intelligence is a fundamental educational factor for participation in democracy. Education for participation requires a process that precedes, surpasses, and goes beyond classrooms; a process aimed at the self-discovery of the person and his environment; one that will reinforce the reasoning capacity for

16

analyzing and judging and will enrich the inner world of each individual through the awareness of his own dignity and that of his neighbor. It is a true process of personalization, that is to say, the strengthening of the human being and his specific qualities—mental, physical, emotional, and social.

Education for participation must involve all environments, from family and classrooms to public service organizations and labor, cultural and recreational centers, stimulating inventiveness, criticism, responsible effort, and creativity.

Without the development of intelligence man cannot participate in social life in a conscious and responsible manner. Participation depends on the thorough development of each individual's potentialities. And the development of intelligence means in itself the development of all human capacities.

History's most important ideal has been that of freedom. Everyone has the right to be free. Intelligence is a tool for freedom. It is an absolutely necessary tool: without intelligence, no one can be free. The human person can be freer by the perfection of his own being, which is gained in the progressive actualization of all his faculties.

For the achievement of these goals, in my opinion, the programs for the Development of Intelligence should, through formal and non-formal educational systems and with the massive utilization of mass media, be based on the following principles:

☐ The programs must be directed to the whole population, with special emphasis on the less favored classes, which are the ones who need more social and educational participation in society for the achievement of their own development;

☐ The action has to be aimed at covering each of the stages of human life. Today knowledge allows us to confirm that our capacities can be developed at any age. Life evolves through

17

the development of skills and it is never too early nor too late for this development;

☐ All programs have to have a rigorous scientific basis in agreement with the most recent findings of research and be supported by the current concept of intelligence which emphasizes its dynamic and evolutionary character-not fixed or predetermined-and on the decisive influence of external stimuli on its development;

☐ The action of the development of human intelligence must be kept totally isolated from political proselytism and from the struggles of political parties;

☐ All the programs should be carried out in terms of each country's concrete realities;

☐ From the beginning the policy and programs implemented have to be projected at international levels so that all nations of the world, without any type of discrimination, can participate in maximizing the cooperative use of available scientific resources, thus progressively achieving the most through development of man's capacities.

In continuous and permanent educational action, both in school and out of school, the programs for the development of intelligence must cover the first six years of life, considered as a special stage, and then continue throughout all educational systems, from kindergarten to the university and later on expand to adulthood.

The development and functioning of the brain during early childhood depends on the quality and quantity of interaction existing between the child and his environment. As it has already been proved with scientific research, sensory-motor experiences are basic for the development of cognitive capacities.

The brain of a newborn is characterized by its immaturity and plasticity. This stimulation is basic for the complete development of the human being's bio-psycho-social potential. A program directed to the first years of life should have as a basic objective to offer *all* children, through their families, the opportunity of achieving a maximum development of their potentialities, from the embryonic stage up to the age of six. The idea is to train parents and other adults surrounding the child in the effective procedures that contribute to the complete development of the child.

The family is the basic cell of society, and as such it must also become the basic cell of the entire educational system, whose focus must then move from the school to the home, having in mind that the pre-school stage starts at pregnancy. Education should start at the moment of conception, with parents acting as teachers. They have in their hands the development of the new men and women in the most important stage of their development. They have to be trained to fulfill this task, the most important one that can be thought of for the benefit of society.

On the other hand, one of the most urgent needs of every country is a deep and thorough reform of its educational system as a whole. The learning of any discipline involves certain basic mental processes that are pre-requisites for the assimilation of knowledge. But these processes are not thoroughly learned in a spontaneous manner; there must be deliberate and systematic teaching and practice of the processes so as to increase thinking skills, learning capacity, and, subsequently, school performance.

Within the formal education system, the programs for the development of intelligence have to incorporate the learning and practice of those mental capacities through methodologies that, besides being a vehicle for cognitive development, can act on other aspects of personality.

19

Contents change, systems remain. The most important educational goal is learning to learn.

Programs for the development of intelligence should be also directed to the adult population that is not part of the country's formal educational system, so as to attain permanent development of each citizen's potential.

Human dignity is the same for everyone: men, women, children, youngsters and old people. Everybody has the right to develop his or her own personality. It is possible to deliberately stimulate and raise the cognitive dimensions of each individual without the limitations of age or educational level.

The purpose of all action to stimulate human potential is that individuals can grow in an attitude of on-going interest in education that will make them respond to society in an independent manner, without submission, within the framework of the integrity of human capacities.

The basic objective of all programs for the development of human intelligence is to offer the benefits of scientific knowledge to all the people of every country, with no discrimination, so that they can participate as main characters in the creation of the future—a future of freedom, democracy, and peace.

Through the development of human intelligence we can achieve that future. Now at the end of the 20th century, this has to be our goal. Our universal goal.

Reuven Feuerstein

"Intelligence is not a static structure, but an open, dynamic system that can continue to develop throughout life!" Dr. Reuven Feuerstein's revolutionary words, not yet widely accepted by the psychological and educational establishments, make an enormous difference in how we perceive the role of education. If intelligence is modifiable, and if indeed intelligence can be taught and learned, education has a much greater role than might have been previously imagined.

Dr. Reuven Feuerstein, a clinical psychologist who studied at the University of Geneva under Jean Piaget, Andre Rey, Barbel Inhelder, and Marguerite Loosli Uster, went on to earn his Ph.D. in Developmental Psychology at the Sorbonne. From 1970 until the present Dr. Feuerstein has served as Professor in the School of Education at Bar Ilan University in Ramat Gan, Israel; he is also the Director of the Hadassah-Wizo-Canada Research Institute, in Jerusalem, Israel.

His life's work has been the development of the Theory of Structural Cognitive Modifiability and its emergent practices of dynamic assessment, active intervention, and placement of both children and adults in "shaping environments."

From 1940-44, Dr. Feuerstein was co-director and teacher in the School for Disadvantaged, Disturbed Children in Bucharest, and from 1945-48 he worked with child survivors of concentration camps. During the 50's, he served as director of Psychological Services of Youth Aliyah in Europe.

There are currently under way over 1,000 research projects on his work throughout the world involving all age groups from infancy to old age, in every setting from jungles to board rooms, and with every ability level from the profoundly retarded to the highly gifted. In 1990 Dr. Feuerstein was decorated by the President of France for his work in training French workers, managers, and executives in the skills of intelligence.

The Hadassah-Wizo-Canada Research Institute, where the theory of Structural Cognitive Modifiability (SCM) and its three applied systems—namely the Learning Potential Assessment Device (LPAD), Instrumental Enrichment (IE), and the Shaping of Modifying Environments—as well as the pivotal theory of Mediated Learning Experience (MLE) have been developed and implemented, is undergoing very meaningful changes in its goals, size, and modality of functioning. The International Center for Learning Potential is being called into life by the dramatic increase in requests for the Institute's service and training programs, which have already become overloaded.

Recognition of the theory of SCM and its associated systems is being used throughout the world in 25 countries. The latest, the 26th, is China, in which the book on IE, written by the author in collaboration with Prof. Yaacov Rand and the late Prof. Mildred Hoffman, has been translated. We are told it is arousing great interest with positive feedback. Chinese scholars in psychology and education consider IE with its underlying theory of SCM to be a useful tool for the needs of hundreds of millions of people in China, confronted as they are now with the need to adapt to changes in technology and in their lifestyle.

The International Center will have three major departments that will dovetail in an integrated manner: Research and Development, Training, and Service. The first, Research and Development, will focus on the further development of instruments and modes of application in response to the particular needs of specific populations. Research will be important for evaluating the results of applying the three systems of the LPAD, IE, and the Shaping of Modifying Environments, and thereby also analyzing feedback in order to define what new development is necessary.

An example of such development is our program for training youngsters with Down's syndrome and learning disabilities to become caregivers to the elderly and handicapped. We developed this project by taking into account a few relevant requirements for a suitable career for such youngsters: first, very limited competition in this field because of the growing great demand for manpower and lower social desirability; second, the consonance of the personality characteristics and abilities of people with learning disabilities, in particular with Down's syndrome, with the requirements of this occupation. After initial doubts, the outcome of our experience has been extremely positive. From an experimental program with 11 students, we have expanded to a framework which will make it possible to include 40 students at a time in the two-year course. Ongoing research will help improve the curriculum and modes of approach, the selection process for candidates, and also the discovery of other suitable occupations for these youngsters that will help them become independent, useful members of society.

Training is the second department. The International Center is partly a response to pressure on the part of hundreds of people seeking longer periods of training than the annual two week International Workshops held over the last 18 years in Jerusalem; this center will offer possibilities to participants to become qualified as trainers of our applied systems in their respective fields. Our method of training people in the theory and its derived techniques has become insufficient for the best possible application of our program. In particular, the growing cross-cultural application requires more access to the theory in order to extend the derivation of universally applicable rules and techniques.

The International Center will incorporate a broad inter-disciplinary team with representatives from education, psychology, neurology, pediatrics, sociology, cultural anthropology, social work, criminology, and auxiliary functions, such as speech, psychotherapy, physiotherapy, and occupational therapy. In the process of working together they will apply the systems and will shape modalities of approach for children and adults who need various applications from these fields of study. Cooperating experts from this wide range of professions will be able to interact, and, with the help of the theory of SCM, develop an all-encompassing approach to benefit children maximally while simultaneously both enriching themselves and those who come for training. These students, similarly coming from this wide professional range, will be oriented in the theory of SCM and will learn how to apply one or more of the related systems and intervention programs while working with children and adults included in our Service department. Those who are interested will be given the chance to participate in research projects.

The International Center will have a close affiliation with a number of universities interested in introducing some of the programs generated by the International Center into their framework. This will enable it to offer academic course credits and dissertation supervision. It is strongly hoped that the International Center will be able to offer stipends and will involve exchanges of faculty and students.

The third department within the International Center, Service, will allow for expansion of the current program at the Institute for directly helping individual children and young adults. This will serve not only for solving problems of the child by offering dynamic assessment and Mediated Learning Experiences, but its work will be coordinated by the other two departments, Research and Development and Training. People coming to train will also become part of the staff giving service.

One of the most rapidly developing areas in the last few years is the application of Mediated Learning and the intervention programs in industry. Especially in France, hundreds of industrial plants, including some of the most prestigious, are using IE and MLE to prepare their manpower for the great technological changes taking place in modern industry. As it was described by the head of a steel mill in Haironville, "We are among the oldest establishments in the field of iron and steel. Three hundred and fifty years of our existence have been marked by very limited change. In the first 300 years, only one technique was used in our industry. In the last fifty years, about ten techniques have been introduced. Now we have to prepare our manpower for techniques which we have not yet even identified. For this, IE (or as it is called in French, PEI) is most helpful." This is true for a very large number of industries, including Thompsons, Peugeot, SNECMÅ, and Hewlett-Packard.

In a conference organized by ASP, an office to coordinate the various programs, that took place at Aix-le-Bains, France, at the end of January, 1990, the different applications of IE and MLE were described by those using them. This conference was headed by the DFD and their directors, M. Dominique Delage and Mlle. Camille Lirot. In another group involved in the application of IE in continuing education at the Sorbonne in Paris, M. Alain Moal and Mme. Sorel are piloting a very interesting approach in which MLE, in conjunction with IE, is being used to shape the curriculum which is offered to adults in continuing education.

Other countries such as Portugal and Spain are interested in using this approach in their industries, not only as preparation for future technologies but also to help those who have become unemployed through the great recent changes in industrial technology. This process requires a total reorientation in these potential workers by mediating those prerequisites of learning that will enable these people to learn the new ways of thinking, perceiving, and functioning necessary for their adaptation.

We have just learned about such an initial course that applies an IE program in a high-tech laboratory in the United States, where until now use of our program in industry has lagged behind Europe. With this first systematic application, we hope to learn about the conditions under which American industry can best benefit from a program meant to develop the self-directed flexibility of workers, reopening them for learning processes and orienting them towards a new way of thinking and a more efficient way of approaching new technology.

The theory of MLE itself is being applied in varied areas. At the Second International Conference on Mediated Learning Experience conducted by Professor Katherine Greenberg, in Knoxville, Tennessee, in the summer of 1989, forty-five lecturers presented their applications of MLE in a great variety of areas ranging from early childhood and children at risk to higher education. Many who teach science to people of the Third World have adopted MLE as a way to prepare them for careers in science. A number of dissertations have recently been published, such as that by Prof. Mehl from South Africa. The theory of MLE is becoming increasingly widely used as a theory of instruction where the need to modify the learner's capacity to learn is the major goal.

The American College Board has become interested in using the dynamic assessment process in the LPAD for people who want to enter college but cannot pass the standard static methods of assessment such as the Scholastic Aptitude Test (SAT). Our more recently developed group LPAD test is becoming recognized as a useful system-oriented approach for group settings such as those school classrooms which are known to have difficulties in promoting their students to higher education. The results of group dynamic assessment, showing the individuals' and the group's profile of modifiability through a mediated test approach, help to reshape the goals of these individuals. There is a great potential with large-scale application of the group LPAD to significantly affect the prospects for higher level of education and occupation of large sectors of disadvantaged populations. In the Third World such development is vital for their economic and social welfare. Large numbers of individuals examined with static measures, such as the IQ or other achievement tests, are doomed to fail and to perpetuate their disadvantaged conditions. For these people only dynamic assessment can reveal their true capacities to learn.

The third applied system, derived from the theory of Structural Cognitive Modifiabililty and now in the process of development, is the Shaping of Modifying Environments. It is mostly a conceptual approach that will enable people to guide those responsible for environments in which children and young adults are educated as to how to shape these environments so as to create the conditions necessary for the individuals' modifiability. Our experience has shown that even if we accurately diagnose the potential for change and then succeed to increase the modifiability of individuals, there is still more to be accomplished. What is crucial is that individuals be surrounded by an environment that enables them to materialize this modifiability. The author and Prof. Jerold Beker from the University of Minnesota are examining precisely what is necessary to turn an environment into a modifying one.

We are hoping that the large group of those who we have already trained will become part of the growing circle of Friends of the International Center to maximize its effort to help those in need through research, training and direct service. The new International Journal for Mediated Learning Experience (Howard Sharron, Editor, 6/7 Hockley Hill, Birmingham B18 5AA, England) will publish ongoing research, international modalities of application and critical review, serving researchers in this field.

Barbara Clark

At New Horizons for Learning's Education Summit Conference on Lifespan Learning in 1988, Dr. Barbara Clark, author of *Growing Up Gifted*, advised, "We must see how what we do affects children so our limits won't be theirs, and we can share their visions. Our mission is to push the limits. We need to look for potential to break through for all children!"

Throughout her career, Dr. Clark has worked to develop ways of teaching children of all ability levels to learn more effectively through holistic educational practices. Her most recent book, *Optimizing Learning*, published in 1986, offers practical, how-to strategies for teaching and learning based on current cognitive research and on the results of the numerous educational programs in which her work has been implemented. Her Integrative Education Model utilizes brain/mind research as the basis for optimizing teaching and learning through exercising thinking, feeling, intuition, and physical sensing in mutually supportive ways.

Dr. Clark is professor in the Division of Special Education at California State University, Los Angeles, where she is coordinator for graduate programs in the area of Gifted Education. Her background is in Special Education for both learning handicapped and gifted students.

As a trustee and director of the Center for Educational Excellence for Gifted and Highly Able Learners, she directed their School Project for seven summers. She serves as vice-president of the National Association for Gifted Children and is a member of the Board of Directors and past president of the California Association for the Gifted. Dr. Clark is a United States delegate to the World Council for Gifted and Talented. She was named Outstanding Professor of 1978-79 at the California State University, Los Angeles.

INTEGRATIVE EDUCATION   Barbara Clark, Ed.D.

The last two decades have brought a tremendous increase in knowledge in nearly every field of study. This knowledge has had important implications for the theory and practice of education. Recent years have brought questions of reform in our schools; of what must be taught, what is effective teaching, and suggestions for techniques and strategies that will promote success for all learners.

Unfortunately, these two events, new knowledge in many disciplines and the movement for reform, have been largely explored as unrelated, ignoring the new information that could help educators better realize their goals for effective teaching and learning. It is the

31

fostering of this relationship that seems critical in the coming decade.

Education must take advantage of new information from other fields on how human learning may be enhanced. As new insights are gained in brain research, cognitive psychology, systems theory, linguistics, and other diverse fields, they must be reflected in the classroom. It was for this purpose of synthesizing current knowledge that the Integrative Education Model was first developed.

Following are some of the promising ideas from other fields that could have important implications for education:

Connectedness, Interrelatedness, and Integration

Connectedness, Interrelatedness, and Integration are common themes found in the research of many fields of study. Neuroscientists show integration and association as the overriding functions of the brain; physicists find connectedness and interrelatedness a critical part of the structure of the universe; linguists promote the "whole language approach"; and systems theorists consider connectedness and interrelatedness as essential to the survival of any system. Implications for education include thematic teaching, multidisciplinarity in presentation of content, reorganization of school and classroom management to include participation and shared responsibility, and integration of all the brain functions in the learning process.

Interdependence of Emotional, Cognitive, Physical, and Intuitive Functions

Interdependence of emotional, cognitive, physical, and intuitive functions allows learners to be effective and efficient when the opportunities are provided for the use of all of these support systems for learning. The neurosciences have brought forth a wide base of support to validate the need for teaching to the whole child. While this concept has been discussed in the past, it must be implemented in the classroom if learners are to be allowed to develop all their talents and skills. Where previously only the cognitive skills that were analytic and linear were considered important, current data show that the integration of all brain functions (analytic *and* gestalt processes of cognition, emotion, physical sensation, and intuition) can better support learning and ensure success to every learner.

Higher Thought Processes, Synthesis, Creativity, and Physical Well-Being

Higher thought processes, synthesis, creativity, and physical well-being are seen to be enhanced by reducing tension and encouraging the use of visualization and imagery. A great many fields now use these methods with positive results. Education needs the support of such findings to bring to students a full actualization of their abilities and to allow them the use of the power of their own minds.

Environmental Concern and Global Awareness

Environmental concern and global awareness are increasing; efforts are being made to incorporate the findings from these areas of study into every discipline. The classroom is not the only place where learning occurs. The environment of the classroom rarely incorporates the richness and diversity of the many cultures and communities of our world; yet learners of today must function in this very diversity and complexity. Learning experiences must be provided beyond the classroom, using the community and the natural environment as sites for learning and teaching.

These are but a few of the issues and ideas current in the knowledge of other disciplines that must impact the reform of our schools. As the implementation and development of the Integrative Education model continues, it becomes more evident that it provides a structure able to bring all these support data into the learning experience. Because the model is based on these data, it holds real promise as an open theory including flexible practices that can easily reflect new information allowing the education of our children to be optimal and dynamic. For these reasons and with this promise in mind, further implementation of the Integrative Education Model will continue to be high priority in the decade to come.

Marian Cleeves Diamond

Also at the 1988 Education Summit Conference, Dr. Marian Diamond delivered the keynote, holding a real human brain in her hand as she spoke. The power of reinforcing teaching with vivid visual examples was never so clear!

Not only is she one of the world's great neuroscientists, but she is a compelling lecturer who knows how to bring information to life for her listeners. She loves teaching and she loves learning and discovery—prime attributes for any teacher who wishes her students to become lifelong learners.

Her most recent book, *Enriching Heredity*, describes Dr. Diamond's lifework of ascertaining that the anatomy of the brain can be changed by the environment. Her studies show conclusively that positive, nurturing, stimulating environments that encourage interaction and response are the prime conditions for developing the more complex neural networks that appear to be the "hardware" of intelligence. Her work also indicates the on-going influence of the environment, experience, learning, and emotions on neural equipment throughout life—for better or worse. In the light of her work, the ageless nature-nurture controversy becomes moot.

Dr. Diamond is professor of Anatomy at the University of California, Berkeley, and Acting Director of the Lawrence Hall of Science. She has also taught at Harvard, Cornell, and at universities in China, Australia, and Africa. She received the Outstanding Teaching Award and Distinguished Teacher's Award from the University of California, and is a member of the American Association of University Women Hall of Fame. In 1989-90, she received the CASE Award, California Professor of the Year, and National Gold Medalist, and she was made a member of the San Francisco Chronicle Hall of Fame.

EDUCATION
IN THE DECADES AHEAD

Marian Cleeves Diamond, Ph.D.

EACH ONE—TEACH ONE is my theme for the coming years. Having just become the Acting Director of the Lawrence Hall of Science here in Berkeley, I want to introduce the concept that everyone can learn to be a teacher. One has to be accurate with the facts as a teacher, yet imaginative with creative ideas for new directions in the future. As we learn the facts, we can turn around and share with the next person so that "the association cortices" can create the new ideas.

A child in kindergarten can learn to be a teacher. The expression on the face of the little ones when they are told they, too, can teach is priceless. They have to reconstruct their image of a teacher. Why spend the next twelve to fifteen years in only being taught? What one learns the first day of school can be shared not only with other schoolmates but with parents as well. Having learned about bones, one child in kindergarten taught his mother that bones are alive. The parent replied this was not so. The child came back to school to reconfirm what he had learned in class and then returned home to correct his parent's misconception. What a mode of education! Everyone benefits as everyone learns.

What is more important is that one learns that she or he has the capacity to learn at *any* age, not only in the classroom during school hours. Life could be a continual learning process as we gain new information and interweave it with the best of the old to improve upon daily conditions for everyone. The outer layers of the brain have the capacity to change positively as well as negatively at any age. As my ninety-five-year-old aunt used to say to me, "Who needs the negative?"

The more we learn about the structure and function of the brain and its potential, the more tolerant we will become of our individual differences and the better able to recognize and accept our similarities. Rather than wonder why we don't understand each other, we can be amazed that we understand each other at all— brain cells are constantly changing with experience.

I hope that basic anatomy and physiology will become a part of the everyday curriculum. If children learned about the wonders of their bodies as healthy little people, they would learn to take care of themselves so that their full 100 years on this globe, and, perhaps, on others as well, could be more optimistic, healthy ones.

The yearly cost of health care in our society is in the billions of dollars, an inexcusable waste, which education could reduce. We could begin early, when the body is the child's world, before reaching out into knowledge about the surrounding environment. If taught to respect himself or herself at the beginning, to learn about the "house" in which she or he will spend a lifetime, then in turn the attitude toward others will be more wholesome and tolerant. There are reasons why such sayings as "know thyself" have been passed along for centuries.

I look forward to working in the Lawrence Berkeley Hall of Science because there is no grading there. Children and adults alike gain knowledge because they are curious. To retain curiosity for a lifetime could be a goal of all teachers, both young and old. At present, teaching first graders is a world apart from teaching tenth graders. The openness and the eagerness of the little ones in contrast to the complacency of many in the older group is truly remarkable. Countless numbers of the older young people have been turned off to the thrill of learning. To keep the excitement of learning and creativity alive at all ages is the ultimate challenge, giving life meaningful color.

It may sound strange in a short article on education to include what I think is the most important ingredient of human behavior, namely love. Why can't we teach the youngsters to love others as they love their families, as an example? Imagine what our daily lives would be like! Somehow in our highly technical world at times the warmth of human compassion seems to be overshadowed by cold efficiency. The exotic sciences of the future might benefit from ecstasies of love in the present.

Noboru Kobayashi

Dr. Noboru Kobayashi, President of the National Children's Hospital in Tokyo, made a memorable presentation at New Horizons for Learning's Creating Our Future in Education Conference in 1987. As a member of the Japanese National Council on Educational Reform, he described his concerns about the current state of education.

Established in 1984, the Council was charged with considering educational reform from a long-term perspective. In 1985, the Council identified eight basic principles for educational reform: greater respect for individuality; emphasis on fundamentals; cultivation of creativity; thinking ability and power of expression; expansion of opportunities for choices; humanization of the educational environment; transition to a lifelong learning system; coping with internationalization; and coping with the information age.

In their 1987 report, the Council identified three goals for education, which Dr. Kobayashi quoted: "(1) the nurture of open and generous hearts and minds, strong bodies and richly creative spirits; (2) the development of free and self-determining spirits and public-minded character; (3) the cultivation of Japanese competent to live as members of the world community."

As Dr. Kobayashi has described the concerns of the Japanese about their educational "state of desolation," it becomes quite clear that educational reform must be a world enterprise.

He has devoted his life to the research and practice of pediatric medicine, with special focus on infant behavior, child ecology, maternal/child health, and school health. He was Professor of Pediatrics and Director of the Pediatric Department at the University of Tokyo in 1970, and in 1984 he established the National Children's Medical Research Center and was the first general director. For twelve years he was president of the International Pediatric Association.

THE EMOTIONAL BASIS
OF LEARNING

Noboru Kobayashi, M.D.

All pediatricians know that when a child is deprived of emotional support in daily life, he or she may be delayed in growth and development physically and mentally. This usually happens in child abuse and other distress, when the parents or the family have problems. This is called "Emotional (or Maternal) Deprivation Syndrome." It is important to know that the deprived child may be able to catch up in growth and development if he or she is provided with emotionally supportive care.

We know that the growth and development of orphans can be

41

influenced by the personality and the character of the people who take care of them. We also know that growth and development of children recovering from severe malnutrition is also determined by emotional factors in addition to nutrition.

These phenomena indicate that the biological program of growth and development present in a child's body is influenced by emotion. Further indications are that programs of growth and development are interacting with programs of both the body and the mind. The situations stated above are considered to be results of dysfunction of the program of the mind, resulting in delay of growth and development.

This is a rather mechanistic and overly rough approach to human development. However, we can say that the body is composed of various "biological systems," and the system is made up of combinations and connections of cells, tissues and organs. These body systems are operated by biological programs, which are composed of sets of genetically determined biological codes. Each program makes its body system function by biological factors, mainly through the nervous system.

As stated above, the biological programs can be divided into two categories, those of body functions, or body programs such as circulation, respiration, and walking, and those of brain function, or mental programs, such as learning, imitation, thinking, believing, or experiencing pleasure, or sadness. Programs of growth and development fine-tune the programs of body and mind so that growth and development of the child are maintained.

Presence of the biological programs can be well demonstrated by studies in fetal and neonatal medicine made possible by recent developments of new technology. Heartbeat can be demonstrated at five or ten weeks after conception by ultrasonic monitoring. This provides evidence that the body system of heart and circulation is already organized and operated by a circulation program at this early stage. The biological program of respiration is well developed at the end of pregnancy, as shown by the respiration-like movements of the thorax of the fetus, but it actually starts to operate with initial respiration just after birth.

The stepping reflex (automatic walk) of the neonate shows that the neonate is able to perform ambulatory-like movement of the lower extremities if the body is well supported. This reflex disappears soon after delivery, however, during the first month or so. The child is born with the program for walking; however, after weightless life in the uterus during the pregnancy the infant's cognitive power of three-dimensional space is limited at birth, and the muscle power of the infant legs is not enough to support the body weight outside the uterus. Thus, the program of walking is switched off by fear of the environment, and then the stepping reflex disappears. The time comes at approximately twelve months, however, when the child develops the cognitive capacity to assess the space and muscle power of the legs to support the body weight, and then the program for walking will be switched on again. This may be the reason why infants can start spontaneously to walk without being taught how to, when they reach the right age.

It may be demonstrated by ultrasonic monitor that the fetus is sucking his/her finger, especially when stimulated by sudden noise. Smiling, crying, and other emotional expressions are developed without instruction or education when the infant reaches a certain age after birth. This indicates programs of the mind are present already at the early stage of life, some even at the fetal stage.

When human beings are talking with each other, of course, they use not only spoken language, but also facial expression and hand and body movements that may be called "behavior language." Verbal and behavior language interact with each other. It can be observed that body movements, facial expression, and movement of the other parts of body such as the hand are synchronized with spoken language in the speaker himself, and even between the

43

speaker and listener. This phenomenon is called "entrainment" in communication. We have made the following experiment with babies:

Hand movements of the neonate were videotaped when a mother was freely saying affectionately to her neonate, "This is mommy, dear," or something like that. The videotaped picture was subjected for quantitative analysis by computer, and the results showed clearly that there was synchronization of the mother's voice and the neonate's movement. This suggests that every neonate has a program for communication.

Of course, we are not robots. The child is born with programs for imitation, learning, thinking, memorizing, and other higher mental functions that take in information from the environment and add it to other programs. These programs can be categorized as programs of education. It is demonstrated that even a neonate can imitate protrusion of the tongue and the facial expression of the mother.

No one teaches a baby how to learn, think, and memorize, so that he or she can develop language and other intellectual activities. The infant begins to do it on his own. It is important to realize, however, that the child can improve various functions through education. This is why children can skip and dance when they enter nursery school. They really improve on the program of walking by information obtained through imitation and learning.

On the basis of these studies, it can be said that the human being is born with various body systems and biological programs, and that these programs are switched on not only by some inner mechanism but also by interaction with the environment, particularly emotionally rich and tender stimuli from daily life. We must provide this warm, loving quality at home and school, so that we can make the most of the innate programs of the child. A child can learn better with the "joie de vivre" that is an essential part of the best kind of education. A positive and emotionally rich environment is not a luxury but actually a necessity for better education in the coming 21st century.

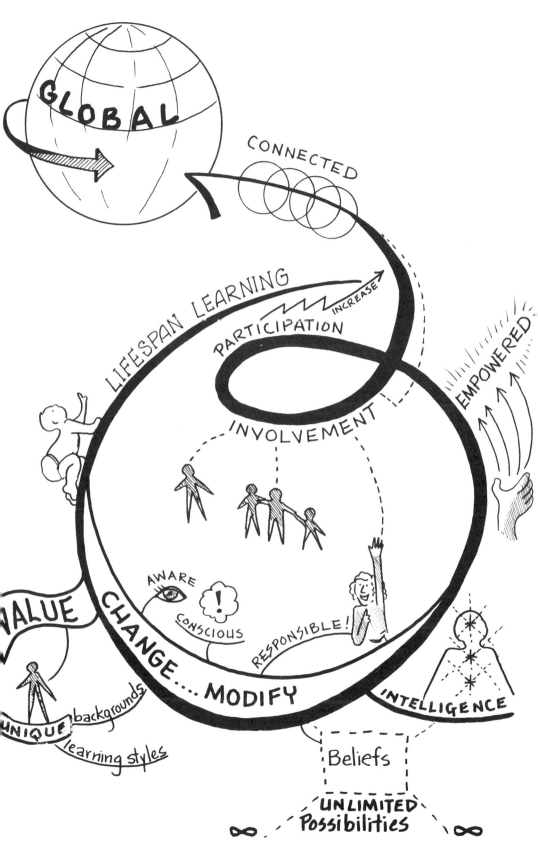

Paul D. MacLean

Dr. Paul MacLean, Senior Research Scientist at the National Institute of Mental Health, has made significant contributions to the understanding the human brain. His work has profound implications for teaching and learning throughout the lifespan, as the following article indicates.

His Triune Brain Theory, based on an evolutionary model of the brain, proposes the idea that the human brain is really three brains in one. The R-Complex is similar to the brain of reptiles, in that it controls basic, instinctive survival thinking and behavior. The limbic system, which is similar to that of lower mammals, seems to be the source of emotions, some aspects of personal identity, and some critically important memory functions. The third and outer formation of the brain, called the neocortex, like the brain of higher mammals, is devoted to higher order thinking skills, reason, linguistic expression, and verbal memory.

MacLean's research suggests that most behaviors are the results of a complex cooperation among these three formations (and systems) of the brain. Of particular significance to educational planning and practice is his finding that when basic needs are not met or there is a negative, threatening emotional context for learning, the brain may literally downshift to basic, survival thinking.

In 1952, he published his first paper on the "visceral brain" and coined the term "limbic system." During an appointment in physiology and psychiatry at Yale he continued to investigate brain mechanisms of emotion, and in 1957 he joined the Laboratory of Neurophysiology at the National Institute of Mental Health, heading a new section on the limbic system. In 1971 he became Chief of the NIMH Laboratory of Brain Evolution and Behavior. An extensive synthesis of his work appears in his book, *The Triune Brain in Evolution*, published in 1990.

EXPANDING LIFESPAN LEARNING   Paul D. MacLean, M.D.

With the celebration of the tenth Anniversary of New Horizons for Learning, it will be one and a half years since New Horizons' memorable Conference on Lifespan Learning at George Mason University. Until being asked to be one of the speakers, I had frankly not thought in terms of lifespan learning. In contemplating this assignment, my first association was to Shakespeare's *As You Like It* and Jaques' lines beginning, "All the world's a stage," and then depicting life's seven ages, or, as one might say, stages. Certainly, Shakespeare's pictures of the last two stages would not qualify as an advertisement for lifespan learning and would not give one iota of support for Browning's exhortation, "Grow old along with me, The best is yet to be, The last of life, for which the first was made!" More about that in a moment.

Since all life's experiences and actions are staged in the brain, I decided to choose as the title of my talk "All the Brain's a Stage." But then in terms of lifespan learning, I began to have second thoughts because of the gnawing question of what to say about Shakespeare's last two ages. I was dissatisfied with the prospect of avoiding the question by focusing on what I considered to be the two most important stages (and in many respects the most neglected) in human learning—namely, the first two stages. That would be a natural focus for me because the latest phase of my research has been concerned with the localization of brain mechanisms accounting for three forms of family-related behavior that characterize the evolutionary transition from reptiles to mammals—namely, 1) maternal nursing and care, 2) audiovocal communication for maintaining maternal-offspring contact, and 3) play. Indeed, one could say that the 180-million-year history of evolution of mammals is the history of the evolution of the family. The very name for mammals is attributable to their possession of mammary glands for nursing. In contrast to reptilian hatchlings, baby mammals could not survive without the nourishment and attentions of a nursing mother. The maternal compulsion to answer to these needs might be regarded as representing the germ of responsibility that in human beings generalizes to become what we call conscience.

In sampling mammalian populations, Calhoun found that the number of members in family groups generally did not exceed twelve, a figure doubtless owing to the number of young that a mother can deliver and sustain. In sampling a large number of mammalian species, one finds that the number of nipples averages about six, and seldom exceeds twelve. Since learning and play have their incipience in the nest, it is evident how early experiences carrying over into childhood and adolescence might influence all of subsequent lifespan learning. The noted paleontologist Alfred Romer once commented that it would be no exaggeration "to say that our modern educational systems all stem from the initiation of nursing by ancestral mammals." Such considerations invite discussion about such educational matters as the role of intimacy in teaching and smaller classrooms.

But what positive thing could one possibly say about the time-worn question of why nature puts people out of commission just about when, through experience and learning, they would be better equipped than ever to provide solutions to life's problems? A recent forecast by the World Health Organization has presented a gloomier outlook than ever for people in Shakespeare's last two stages. At the present time more than 10% of the population over sixty years of age suffer from some form of dementia. Based on current statistics, the number of people over sixty will have increased to over one billion by the year 2025. This means that if the present rate of population growth continues, the number of people with senile dementia, Alzheimer's disease, or other cerebral disease will be staggering.

In the past it has been tacitly assumed that because of genetic and other factors not much can be done to alter the aging process. Consequently, society has the expectation that when a person reaches a certain age, he or she becomes suddenly incompetent and, like a dog, is supposed to roll over and make room for a younger individual. No wonder there is so often shriveling depression and a drying-up of the brain's energizing sap! One might say, therefore, that old age is in no small part a *sociogenic disease.*

Until modern times it would seem that nature has never had to deal extensively with human aging. But since 1920 the average life expectancy has increased from fifty-four years to seventy-five. More and more, it is beginning to look as though a number of presumed aging processes are attributable to such causes as slow viral infections, environmental toxins, and dietary factors. The suspicion is growing, for example, that Parkinson's disease, now affecting younger age groups, may be owing to some environmental toxin. Despite the natural blood brain barrier, there are several ways that viruses and toxic agents can get through it to affect the brain.

As mentioned, dietary factors may be involved. It has been recognized that fatty products containing cholesterol may build up in the walls of blood vessels and decrease the blood supply to vital organs. But it is only now being realized that an oversupply of fat in any form may be damaging. This is of particular interest because of the long-time recognition that cellular accumulation of a fatty pigment called lipofuscin (literally, dusky fat) is the most common sign of aging. Lipofuscin is so resistant to analysis that it is still not known how it is formed or exactly what it is made of. Nerve cells are particularly prone to its accumulation because of having no means of getting rid of it. Somewhat analogous to the pile-up of plastic bags of garbage in New York during a strike, packets of lipofuscin may gradually fill up nerve cells until they burst open like seed pods.

Granted that the role of dietary fat in the formation of lipofuscin is not known, the thought suggests itself that one of the reasons the Chinese are valued in old age is because they have a preserved intellect for communication. This recalls that the Chinese diet contains only 15% fat, as opposed to a Western diet of 40% fat. Experimentally, it has long been known that rats raised on a barely subsistent diet may have an increased life expectancy of 30 to 35%. This would mean that if a like outcome could be achieved in human beings, life expectancy could increase to 100 years.

Some pundits would claim that in the past, when there was a relatively short life expectancy, we were victimized by young people who believed they had to do or die before the age of forty or fifty.

Hence, with current life-expectancy, if aging might bring the learning experience and wisdom for more meaningful survival of humanity and the rest of earthly life, there would exist an urgent need to proceed with all haste to learn how the brain could better protect itself and cleanse itself of injurious substances. Such knowledge might prove to be a crucial next step in evolution.

Jane M. Healy

Dr. Jane Healy's first book, *Your Child's Growing Mind*, has in a few short years become a classic reference and guide for parents. Based on recent research in developmental neuropsychology, her book discusses the development of language, intelligence, and memory, along with academic skills.

It has been a major contribution in explaining the dangers of pushing academically demanding subjects down into the early years, when many children are not yet physically or psychologically able to cope with them. Her most recent book, *Endangered Minds*, carries the theme even further, as she discusses other current pressures which may limit human development—and what can be done about them.

Dr. Healy graduated from Smith College and received her master's degree from John Carroll University. She holds a doctorate in educational psychology from Case Western Reserve University, and has engaged in postdoctoral studies at Columbia Teachers' College and Boston Children's Hospital.

She has been a classroom teacher and learning specialist, and is currently on leave from the Hathaway Brown School, where she is Coordinator of Learning Services. At present she is in private practice as an educational therapist and learning consultant in Vail, Colorado. She is also an Adjunct Assistant Professor at Cleveland State University.

In addition to the two books previously mentioned, Dr. Healy has another in press entitled *Whose Brain is Growing Today?* She has written chapters in a number of books, has published many articles and reviews, and is in great demand as a consultant and speaker. She received the Hathaway Brown School Distinguished Alumna Award and the Delta Kappa Gamma 1988 Educator's Award.

ENDANGERED MINDS   Jean M. Healy, Ph.D.

Meaningful learning—the kind that will equip our children and our society for the uncertain challenges of the future—occurs at the intersection of developmental readiness, curiosity, and significant subject matter. Yet many of today's youngsters, at all socio-economic levels, are blocked from this goal by detours erected in our culture, schools, and homes. Fast-paced lifestyles, coupled with heavy media diets of visual immediacy, beget brains misfitted to traditional modes of academic learning. In a recent survey, teachers in both the United States and Europe reported overwhelmingly that today's students have shorter attention spans, are less able to reason analytically, to express ideas verbally, and to attend to complex problems. Meanwhile, school curricula modes of instruction do little to remedy the deficits by engaging either attention or curiosity. The result? A growing educational "crisis" of misfit between children and their schools.

Narrowing the gap between the school's demands and the "readiness" of the students' brains can be accomplished in two ways: changing the student and/or changing the classrooms. Both are possible. Let's start with the students.

Shaping the Malleable Mind
_____

The brain's functioning—and thus its "readiness" for any type of learning—is shaped by both intrinsic and extrinsic factors. Genetic nature combines with prenatal nurture to endow the infant brain with a range of possibilities, but the environment after birth helps forge the neuronal connections that underlie later learning. Like a sculptor, the child's experience prunes away unneeded—or unused—synapses, while strengthening those patterns of connections that are repeatedly used. Thus habits of the mind may become, quite literally, structures of the brain. Although the susceptible cell groups comprise but a small proportion of total brain mass, they are critical to learning because they facilitate higher-level thinking, planning, and skills of mental organization so essential to self-directed and meaningful human learning.

While our understanding of this phenomenon of "neural plasticity," or malleability, of the growing brain is still rudimentary, several principles suggest themselves from the research. First, repeated experiences cause synaptic differences if they comprise a significant part of a child's mental life. For example, the brains of deaf children, or of those otherwise deprived of oral language experience, develop differently from those of hearing children because of differences in the dominant types of input to which they have responded. As yet no one has attempted to demonstrate less dramatic brain changes from a heavy diet of video and rushed, adult-directed activities or from immersion in thoughtful conversation and spontaneous creative play, but it is eminently possible that they exist. (Certainly, anecdotal information from teachers suggests that there has been a shift in information-processing abilities of children in recent years.)

Secondly, animal research and common sense converge on the notion that a brain which is actively involved and curious is likely to develop stronger connections than one which is merely a passive recipient of learning. Third, there appear to be critical, or at least "sensitive" periods in the course of development when certain neuron groups become particularly amenable to stimulation. If sufficient mental exercise is lacking, the related ability may be permanently degraded. This phenomenon has been demonstrated for basic aspects of human language development; very little is known, however, about its applicability to most human learning, particularly the higher-level skills (e.g., understanding of more complex syntax, abstract and analytic reasoning, self-generated attention) which may have sensitive periods well into adolescence. In today's world, these skills appear to be particularly endangered.

So, how do we change the children? First, we stop blaming them—and their teachers. Parents, policy-makers, and the arbiters of popular culture are also part of the the problem. If we wish to retain the benefits of literate thought, we must educate parents, encourage more constructive uses of media, and set our priorities in every classroom to show children from the earliest years how to get ideas into words and to listen—not only to peers and to adults, but also to the voice of an author. I would suggest that every home and every school institute a "curriculum" for listening and following sequential directions, as well as emphasizing the use of language to talk through problems, to plan behavior, and to reason analytically about such concepts as cause and effect. Deficits in these fundamental "habits of mind" cause not only academic but also social problems. Reading instruction should take a back seat until language foundations and skills of auditory analysis and comprehension are in place, lest reading become a meaningless exercise.

Someone must also take time to listen to the children, soften the frenetic scheduling of their lives, read to them, give them some quiet time to play, to ponder, to reflect, and to use the inner voice that mediates attention and problem-solving. Without adult models, children cannot shape their own brains around these intellectual habits which, in the long run, will be far more valuable to all concerned than a frantic march through content. The executive, or pre-frontal, centers of the brain, which enable planning, follow-through, and controlled attention along with forms of abstract thought, develop throughout childhood and adolescence. We have a responsibility to children—all children—to demonstrate the habits of mental discipline and attention necessary to reflect on, utilize, and apply the information they learn. If the culture refuses to cooperate by providing models outside of school, we must add it to our academic curriculum – even if it means sacrificing some of the data in the syllabus.

Since each brain's developmental timetable is different, we must also disabuse ourselves of the notion that children can be *made* to learn on a set schedule. And, finally, we should recognize that whoever is minding the children is shaping our national intelligence—and choose and reward these persons accordingly.

Expanding Minds for a New Century

Merely reinstating some of the mental habits of a bygone era will not suffice, however. We must also accept and capitalize on the fact that today's children come with new skills for a new century. The changes we observe in our children may, in fact, represent a cusp of change in human intelligence—a progression into more immediate, visual, and three-dimensional forms of thought. Schools will need to accept the fact that lectures and "teacher talk," which commonly comprise approximately 90% of classroom discourse, must give way to more effective student involvement. Today's learners must become constructors of knowledge rather than passive recipients of information that even the least intelligent computer can handle more effectively. Many examples already exist in outstanding literature-based programs that turn students on to reading, writing, and oral communication, "hands-on" science and math curricula in which product takes a back seat to understanding of process; project-oriented, multidisciplinary social studies units; cooperative learning paradigms; multi-modal teaching; training of teachers in open-ended questioning.

Particularly exciting are curricular innovations in which the unlimited potential of visual thinking is used to complement language and linear analysis. Courses in critical viewing and effective use of visual media are examples; computer simulations requiring step-by-step progression to three-dimensional reasoning herald development of new skills which may eventually transcend the linear constraints of scientific method and even unite the talents of the two cerebral hemispheres in expanded modes of thought.

Traditional parameters of learning must be broadened, even re-defined, not simply because of the changing priorities of future technologies, but also because of present realities. Our growing crisis in academic learning reflects societal neglect of the neural imperatives of childhood. We find an alienation of children's worlds—and the mental habits engendered by them – from the traditional culture of academia. Merely lamenting this fact, however, does not alter the reality or rebuild the brains. Nor does choking our young with more didacticism—under the rubric of "competency" —make them learn to think. In past decades we got away with insignificant subject matter and poor pedagogy because the culture dutifully sent us docile minds, well-endowed with the linguistic currency of academic learning. But our children today have been differently prepared, and, sophisticated consumers that they are, do not suffer drivel lightly–nor should they.

Closing the gap between wayward synapses and intellectual imperatives will not be accomplished by low-level objectives, such as memorization and recapitulation of information. Human brains are not only capable of acquiring knowledge; they also hold the potential for wisdom. But wisdom has its own curriculum: conversation, thought, imagination, empathy, reflection. Youth who lack these "basics," who have forgotten how to ask the questions that may never have been asked, who cannot ponder what they have learned, are poorly equipped to become managers of our accelerating human enterprise.

The final lesson of neural plasticity is that a human brain, given good foundations, can continue to adapt and expand for a lifetime. Its vast synaptic potential at birth can bend itself around what is important of the "old" and still have room for new skills demanded by a new century. A well-nourished mind, well-grounded in the precursors of wisdom as well as of knowledge, will continue to grow, learn, develop—as long as it responds to the prickling of curiosity. Perhaps this quality, above all, is the one we should strive to preserve in our children. With it, supported by language, thought, and imagination, minds of the future will shape themselves around new challenges—whatever they may be. But if we continue to neglect either these foundations or the curiosity that sets them in motion, we will truly all be endangered.

David Perkins

Dr. David Perkins is concerned with what he calls "the new science of learnable intelligence." He calls learnable intelligence "mindware" because he believes that it is the organization tools of the mind that allow us to be effective. According to Dr. Perkins, the pure practice of intellectual activities results in entrenchment of old patterns that add no improvement in performance.

An entertaining and thought-provoking presenter at our conferences, Dr. Perkins has offered educators new perspectives on the roots of intelligence. Having received his Ph.D. in mathematics and artificial intelligence from the Massachusetts Institute of Technology, he became a founding member of Project Zero at Harvard, and since 1971 has served as co-director of the project.

He participated in the design and testing of a course to teach thinking skills at the seventh grade level in Venezuela for their Intelligence Project. Published in English under the title *Odyssey*, it proved to be highly effective and is now being used in numbers of middle schools in the United States.

As an associate of the Educational Technology Center at the Harvard Graduate School of Education, he undertook research leading to the development of supplementary materials that enhance students' learning of computer programming. He is currently involved in the design of interventions that integrate the teaching of thinking with subject-matter learning. One project focuses on algebra, while another, called Connections, provides elementary school teachers with a systematic approach to integrating key thinking skills across several disciplines.

Dr. Perkins has been a speaker and consultant to educational groups throughout the world and is a consultant to Langley Field NASA and the Los Alamos National Laboratories. In August, 1984, he organized the Conference on Thinking held at the Harvard Graduate School of Education.

MINDWARE AND THE METACURRICULUM

D. N. Perkins, Ph.D.

What Is Intelligence "Made Of?"

One of the most fundamental questions that can be asked about intelligence is: "What is intelligence made of?" That is, what in the human mind and brain leads us to think and act more intelligently? Is intelligence simply a more efficient nervous system? Is it a matter of knowing a lot? Is it being a reflective thinker?

All these factors and more certainly appear to contribute to day-to-day intelligent behavior. Yet many people are dogged "nativists." That is, they believe that "real" human intelligence is entirely innate. You are born with certain neural equipment, that neural equipment has a certain mental horsepower measured by IQ tests, and this is the horsepower you have to work with for the whole of your life. Many people believe there is no such thing as becoming more intelligent in any fundamental sense. To be sure, anyone can learn a great deal of practical value in accordance with his or her abilities. But getting smarter in a basic sense? No.

A fundamental challenge to this nativist position has developed in recent years among educators and psychologists. Many are coming to the conclusion that intelligence is, to a substantial degree, learnable. In addition to accumulating knowledge and skills, people can in a fully real and powerful sense become more intelligent.

Neural, Experiential, and Reflective Intelligence

Not everyone agrees on this point. Indeed, a battle has raged among psychologists for several decades about the true nature of intelligence. Some psychologists consider intelligence a matter of the efficiency of the nervous system, genetically determined, not very subject to environmental influence, and adequately measured by IQ tests. They advocate what might be called a *neural view* of intelligence. Other psychologists have argued that highly intelligent behavior always occurs in a specialty. It involves expertise in a particular area of endeavor, such as violin playing, carpentry, or physics. They advocate what might be called an *experiential view* of intelligence. Experience and its cumulative lessons count for more than anything else. Still other psychologists emphasize how good thinking depends on good mental management—knowing what questions to ask yourself, using problem-solving strategies, monitoring and striving to direct and improve your own thinking. They advocate what might be called a *reflective view* of intelligence.

Considered in perspective, the debate appears somewhat misplaced. Proponents of each camp are trying to lay claim to the "one true intelligence," when there is no particular reason to believe that intelligent behavior has a single cause. Indeed, each camp has compelling arguments for the influence of the factors it highlights. It is time to accept this reality and acknowledge that intelligence is not monolithic. Intelligence has multiple principal causes.

I suggest a framework that recognizes three basic dimensions to intelligence: the neural dimension, the experiential dimension, and the reflective dimension. Rather than rivals, these three should be considered contrasting causal factors that all contribute substantially to intelligent behavior. Such a formulation dissolves a fruitless debate and sets the stage for asking what education can do to cultivate these three dimensions of intelligence.

Of them all, reflective intelligence offers the best target of opportunity for education because reflective intelligence is the most learnable of the three. Research evidence suggests that the neural component of intelligence does not change very much with instruction or practice, although there are nutritional and maturational effects. Experiential intelligence in a particular area takes years to build. But better practices of mental management, strategy use, and metacognition can be cultivated in much shorter periods—not overnight, but in months rather than years, years rather than decades.

Mindware

If reflective intelligence is the target of opportunity, then we should examine its nature more deeply. What is it "made of?" Is it a bag of tricks, a bundle of attitudes, a repertoire of habits?

All those things and more. One encompassing way to describe reflective intelligence is to say that it is made of "mindware." Just as kitchenware consists in tools for working in the kitchen, and software consists in tools for working with your computer, mindware consists in tools for the mind. A piece of mindware is anything a person can learn—a strategy, an attitude, a habit—that extends the person's general powers to think critically and creatively.

Mindware does three jobs, all of which concern the organization of thought. It works to *pattern, repattern, and depattern* thinking. Concerning patterning, a student may not have an organized approach to, for example, writing an essay. There are a number of strategies that help to *pattern* the writing process, not in rigid ways but in flexible and fruitful ways. As to repatterning, a person may suffer from bad thinking or learning practices. For example, many students adopt the strategy of reading something over and over as a way of understanding and remembering it. Research shows that this is not in fact a very effective strategy. Students need to *repattern* their reading, adopting more powerful strategies.

As to depatterning, a person may suffer from overly rigid or narrow ways of approaching problems and managing situations. For instance, people display a strong tendency to look at situations in one-sided ways. Also, people generally fail to question their tacit assumptions. Brainstorming, assumption identification, and other tactics of exploratory thinking can help people to *depattern* their thinking, opening it up to more possibilities and evading the ruts of habit and prejudice.

Practice Does Not Make Perfect

While the notion of mindware to pattern, repattern, and depat-tern thinking may sound like inevitable common sense, it actually strikes a sharp contrast with a common misconception about developing thinking: the "practice makes perfect" notion. Many efforts to cultivate thinking do little more than encourage youngsters

to engage in a lot of hit-or-miss attempts at thinking, through collaborative learning activities, class discussions, project work, and so on.

Such initiatives are fine as far as they go. Certainly we should
applaud any effort to make classrooms more thoughtful settings.
Surely this is a necessary condition for any progress in this promising
area of learnable intelligence. But necessary conditions are not
always sufficient conditions. In this case, there is reason to believe
that practice alone is not enough. Indeed, mere practice can lead
youngsters to entrench their old patterns of thinking rather than
repatterning and depatterning to develop more effective thinking.

This is where *reflective* intelligence truly lives up to its name.
Mere practice is not a very reflective process. In contrast, activities
in which people think about their thinking, learn good ways of
patterning, repatterning, and depatterning, and adapt this
"mindware" to their own needs or even invent their own mindware,
are much more likely to develop thinking. Better thinking typically
means not just smoother, faster thinking, which practice alone would
yield, but fundamentally reorganized thinking, which requires
pointblank attention to mindware.

Toward the Metacurriculum

The examples of mindware that I have given so far are rather
general. What about the subject matters? Many psychologists have
argued in recent years that general skills of thinking are no substitute
for knowledge in particular subject matters.

I agree with this strongly. Moreover, each subject matter
brings with it not only important "content" to master but its own
specialized mindware. For example, any discipline has problem-
solving strategies of special importance to it—in physics, such
methods as energy balance equations; in literature, attention to
fundamental dimensions of stories such as plot, character, and
setting; in writing, such strategies as free writing; and so on.

65

Likewise, any discipline has its distinctive ways of explaining and justifying ideas, ways which differ somewhat from subject matter to subject matter. Mathematics highlights formal deductive proof; the sciences emphasize empirical evidence from experiments; history depends on evidence from primary sources; and so on. In summary, every discipline has its distinctive "mindware," consisting of those problem-solving strategies, ways of validating ideas, and other practices that help to pattern, repattern, or depattern thinking in fruitful ways.

Unfortunately, what schools principally teach is a curriculum of content—the facts and procedures of a subject matter. Over-whelmingly, textbooks purvey the facts of history, the algorithms of arithmetic, the formulas of science. There is little explicit attention either to general purpose mindware or to the distinctive mindware for each of the subject matters. What is missing, one might say, is the *metacurriculum*—the "higher order" curriculum that deals with good patterns of thinking in general and in the subject matters.

How, then, to develop such mindware in students? One solution is to offer special courses focused on the art of thinking. In my view, well-designed interventions of this sort are worthwhile. But they are not likely to prove feasible on a wide scale in the already crowded school curriculum. And they are not enough. Abundant research shows that the subject matters desperately need a direct injection of thoughtfulness, a "mindware booster shot." I am an advocate of what is often called *infusion*—integrating the teaching of new concepts in a deep and far-reaching way with subject matter instruction.

The challenge to education therefore becomes one of envisioning, articulating, and bringing alive the metacurriculum to go with the curriculum. Appropriate mindware for mathematics should be as much of a presence in the mathematics classroom as are number facts or the quadratic equation. Thoughtfulness about how we know and test historical claims should be as much of a presence in the history classroom as the story of the U.S. Civil War. The marriage of curriculum and metacurriculum can provide students with the mindware to make the subject matters more understandable, thought-provoking, and connected with their lives.

Howard Gardner

In 1981 Dr. Howard Gardner was awarded a MacArthur Prize Fellowship in support of Project Zero at Harvard University. An announcement of the award quoted Gardner as saying early in his career, that he had been a committed Piagetian, but as he pursued his own studies he came to view Piaget's theories as "too narrow a notion of how the human mind works."

He noted further that he didn't believe there was "one form of cognition which cuts across all human thinking. There are multiple intelligences with autonomous intelligence capacities." This statement heralded the writing of his book *Frames of Mind,* which was published in 1983.

Dr. Gardner's Theory of Multiple Intelligences, described in this seminal book, has become the framework for many of the effective educational strategies currently being implemented to expand human development. All the conferences presented by New Horizons for Learning have been produced with that theory in mind—presenting new information through all the intelligences.

Gardner's Theory of Multiple Intelligences proposes that people use at least seven relatively autonomous intellectual capacities – to approach problems and create products. These include linguistic, musical, logical-mathematical, spatial, bodily-kinesthetic, interpersonal, and intrapersonal intelligences.

He suggests that "although they are not necessarily dependent on each other, these intelligences seldom operate in isolation. Every normal individual possesses varying degrees of each of these intelligences, but the ways in which intelligences combine and blend are as varied as the faces and the personalities of individuals."

Dr. Gardner is professor of Education and co-director of Project Zero at the Harvard Graduate School of Education. He is also a research psychologist at the Boston Veterans Administration Medical Center and adjunct professor of Neurology at the Boston University School of Medicine.

INTELLIGENCE IN SEVEN STEPS   Howard Gardner, Ph.D.

The concept of intelligence, a very old one, has been employed in the most varied ways over the centuries. During the past century, there has been considerable movement on the "intelligence front," and this trend shows no sign of abating. In this essay I briefly describe seven historical steps, or phases, in the development of thinking about intelligence, focusing in particular on work inspired by the Theory of Multiple Intelligence.

Lay Conceptions

Until this century, the word "intelligence" has been used primarily by ordinary individuals in an effort to describe their own mental powers as well as those of other persons. Consistent with ordinary language usage, "intelligence" has been deployed in anything but a precise manner. Forgetting about homonyms which denote the gathering of information, individuals living in the West were called "intelligent" if they were quick or eloquent or scientifically astute or wise. In other cultures, the individual who was obedient, or well behaved, or quiet, or equipped with magical powers, may well have been referred to by terms which have been translated as "intelligent."

For the most part, the word "intelligent" was used in a beneficent way; however, its imprecision can be readily displayed by a recognition that it has been applied to nearly all of the American presidents in this century, even though it is doubtful that any two of our presidents exhibited similar kinds of minds. Perhaps ironically, Herbert Hoover and Jimmy Carter, two of Americas least successful presidents, both of whom were engineers, probably came closest to the lay idea of "intelligence." It may be worth noting that they have become distinguished by their behaviors as *ex*-presidents.

The Scientific Turn

In a sequence of events that is by now familiar, Alfred Binet responded to requests from Parisian ministers at the turn of the century by creating the first intelligence test. It then became possible to estimate an individual's "intelligence" by noting his or her performance on a deliberately heterogeneous set of items, ranging from sensory discrimination to vocabulary knowledge. Used first clinically for "at risk" Parisian elementary schoolchildren, the intelligence test became "normed" on Californian middle-class children and was administered quite widely, thanks in large part to the efforts of Lewis Terman at Stanford University. By the 1920's and 1930's, intelligence tests (and their product, an individual's IQ) had become deeply ensconced not only in American society but also in many other parts of the world.

Pluralization of Intelligence

While intelligence was initially perceived as a unitary (if overarching) concept, which could be captured by a single number, a debate soon arose about whether the concept could legitimately be broken into components. Such researchers as L.L. Thurstone and J.P. Guilford argued that intelligence was better conceived of as a set of possibly independent factors. In recent years, buoyed by findings from fields as disparate as artificial intelligence, developmental psychology, and neurology, a number of investigators have put forth the view that the mind consists of several independent modules or "intelligences."

In my own "theory of multiple intelligences," I argue that human beings have evolved to be able to carry out at least seven separate forms of analysis: 1) Linguistic intelligence (as in a poet); 2) Logical-mathematical intelligence (as in a scientist); 3) Musical intelligence (as in a composer); 4) Spatial intelligence (as in a sculptor or airplane pilot); 5) Bodily kinesthetic intelligence (as in an athlete or dancer); 6) Interpersonal intelligence (as in a salesman or teacher); 7) Intrapersonal intelligence (exhibited by individuals with accurate views of themselves). These ideas have attracted some attention on the part of educators seeking a more comprehensive and individualized educational system. Recently my colleagues and I have been exploring certain educational implications of the theory in our own research.

Contextualization

As initially put forth, most theories of intelligence—whether singular or multiple—have assumed that intelligences are simply biological entities or potentials, which exist "in the head" (and "in the brain") and can be measured reliably, independent of context. While the theory of multiple intelligences was deliberately formulated to take into account the unfolding of intelligence in different cultures, it nevertheless suffered in its early formulations from an "individual-centered" bias. Most students of intelligence, however, are now coming to the realization that intelligence cannot be conceptualized, or measured with accuracy, independent of the particular contexts in which an individual happens to live, work, and play, and of the opportunities and values provided by that milieu. Bobby Fischer might inherently have had the potential to be a great chess player, but if he had lived in a culture without chess, that potential would never have been manifested, let alone actualized. Intelligence is always an interaction between biological proclivities and opportunities for learning in a particular cultural context.

Project Spectrum, a curriculum-and-assessment project for young children, is one reflection of this view. We initially designed the project to determine whether young children exhibit distinctive profiles of intelligences, but we soon came to realize that intelligences could not be measured in the abstract; instead we had to create new environments, contexts more like children's museums than like traditional schoolrooms, in which children's intellectual proclivities had an opportunity to be elicited and practiced. Only then could some kind of meaningful assessment become possible.

Intelligence As Distributed

Closely related to the trend toward the contextualization of intelligence is the realization that significant parts of intelligence are *distributed*. The essential insight here is, again, that not all intelligence is in the head. But rather than residing simply in the general context wherein a person lives, much of everyday intelligence can be located in the human and non-human resources with which individuals work, and on which they come to depend in their productive work. Typically these resources are thought of as non-human artifacts, such as books, notebooks, computer files, and the like. And it is true that in a literate world, much on which the productive individual depends inheres in these materials.

It is also appropriate, however, to think of other individuals as part of one's "distributed intelligence." Most workers do not depend exclusively on their own skills and understanding; rather, they assume the presence of others in their work environments with whom they can regularly interact. This view is brought home vividly when one considers an office that is being computerized. Rarely does all relevant knowledge reside with a single individual; much more commonly, different office members exceed the novice level in different areas of hardware or software expertise. In our terms, intelligence about computers is "widely distributed" across individuals under such circumstances.

Our own efforts to examine the "distributed nature" of intelligence can be seen in two of our projects. In Arts Propel, a cooperative project in arts and humanities assessment, we ask students to keep detailed "processfolios" – complete records of their involvement in a project, from initial conception through interim sketches and drafts, ultimately to new plans that grow out of the final completed project. We believe that students' learning is significantly enhanced when they can have an on-going dialogue with the record of their previous efforts, as captured in these constantly evolving processfolios.

73

In the Key School, an Indianapolis elementary school, children are exposed each day to contexts that nurture each of the intelligences. As part of their regular work at this experimental public school, students carry out each year three theme-related projects. Our research interest is in developing methods whereby these projects can be evaluated in a fair and comprehensive way. Part of that evaluation centers on the ways in which participation in a project has been cooperative: the human and non-human resources involved in preparation of the project, the help given by others in the presentation of the project, and the reactions of other individuals— peers as well as experts—to the final project. By deliberately including these "extra-individual" elements in our evaluations, we hope to bring home to the community the importance of "distributed aspects of intelligence." At the same time we want to undercut the common notion that all skill and learning must exist within a single brain, be that brain at home, at school, or at the work place.

Thus far, I have spoken of historical "steps" that have already been traversed, or which at least are being taken at the present time. My last two "steps" represent hopes for future work on intelligence in our own laboratory and in others around the world.

Nurturance of Intelligence

Even though our efforts to understand intelligence have been advancing, we still know very little about how to nurture intelligence, be it conceptualized in unitary or pluralistic fashion, in individual-centered, contextualized, or distributed form. Yet surely our efforts to understand intelligence as scientists can best be crowned by a demonstration that intelligence can be nurtured in particular educational settings, using strategic pedagogical or facilitating techniques. Here lies one important challenge for the future.

Humanizing Intelligence

Understanding the nature of the human mind in all of its complexity is no mean feat, and a complete understanding may well exceed human investigative capacities. But understanding intelligence—and even knowing how better to develop it—does not suffice in itself. Any human capacity can be used for ill as well as for good; and it is part of our responsibility as human beings living on a single troubled planet to try to use our competences, our intelligences, in morally responsible ways. This assignment cannot fall exclusively on the shoulders of researchers; nor can we simply afford to pass this responsibility on to others.

The human being is also more than his or her intellectual powers. Perhaps more crucial than intelligence in the human firmament are motivation, personality, emotions, and will. If we are ever to obtain a comprehensive and fully integrated picture of human beings, we need to meld our insights about cognition with comparable insights in respect to these other aspects of the human being. Perhaps, indeed, a different view of human nature will result from this activity of synthesis.

Obviously so grand an undertaking requires the highest degree of "distributed collaboration" among researchers, educators, and the general citizenry. Although the task is formidable, the advances made in understanding over the past decade give one some reason for optimism.

Robert J. Sternberg

Another theory of intelligence is proposed by Dr. Robert Sternberg. His Triarchic Theory of Intelligence views individual differences from yet another, but highly complementary, perspective. He points out, as does Dr. Gardner, that traditional educational systems value "componential" intelligence most highly, and that tests are designed largely to assess this type of intelligence— composed primarily of linguistic and logical-mathematical abilities. Two other kinds of intelligence, "contextual" (the source of creative insight) and "experiential" (the "street smarts" of intelligence) are of enormous value to society, yet not reinforced nor given much opportunity to develop in many traditional classrooms. Dr. Sternberg's wit and playful sense of humor keep his audiences laughing as he presents powerful information and practical suggestions for educating students more broadly for a world in great need of creative thinkers and those who enjoy completing tasks to the best of their ability.

Currently IBM Professor of Psychology and Education at Yale University, Dr. Sternberg graduated from Yale and received his Ph.D. in psychology from Stanford University. He has been the winner of numerous awards, including the Early Career Award and Boyd R. McCandless Award of the American Psychological Association, the Outstanding Book and Research Review Awards of the Society for Multivariate Experimental Psychology, and the Distinguished Scholar Award of the National Association for Gifted Children. He is a past winner of National Science Foundation and Guggenheim Fellowships. He received the Mensa Education and Research Foundation Award for Excellence in 1989 and is listed in Science Digest as one of 100 "Top Young Scientists in the United States." He received the Citation Classic Designation of the Institute for Scientific Information and the Outstanding Book Award of The American Educational Research Association.

TRIARCHIC ABILITIES TEST   Robert Sternberg, Ph.D.

During the last ten years, a number of exciting developments have occurred in the domain of theory with respect to our understanding of intelligence. New theories of the mind, such as Howard Gardner's and my own, have expanded our thinking about intelligence and, I believe, helped us realize that intelligence is a much broader construct than many of us had thought. But developments on the measurement front have not, as of yet, kept up with theoretical developments.

It is one thing to propose a new and glitzy theory, but quite another to devise measurement operations that enable educators to assess the abilities posited by the theory in a reliable and valid way. Many theories—of intelligence and of other constructs—have eventually been consigned to the dustheaps of history because the theories were never followed up with measurements that met even the minimal psychometric criteria for a usable test.

One of the most exciting projects in which I am currently involved is the development of the Sternberg Triarchic Abilities Test (STAT). Working with a large and highly regarded test publisher, The Psychological Corporation, I am trying to put into practice what I have been preaching over the past several years.

The STAT, to be published in 1992, will be divided into nine multiple levels for differing ages, and will be suitable for group administration to individuals in kindergarten through college, as well as to adults. Two forms of the test will be available. The test differs in its scope from conventional tests. For one thing, it yields separate scores for componential information processing (analytical ability), coping with novelty (synthetic ability) and (as a separate score) automatization and practical-intellectual skills. Thus, the scores provided by the test correspond strictly to the aspects of intelligence specified by my Triarchic Theory. The theory specifies that intelligence can be understood in terms of components of information processing being applied to relatively novel experience and later being automatized in order to serve three functions in the environment: adaptation to, selection of, and shaping of that environment.

Crossed with these scores are scores for three content areas: verbal, quantitative, and figural. Thus, the various kinds of processing are each measured in each of the three content domains, yielding $4 \times 3 = 12$ separate subtests per level. In this way, it is possible to diagnose not only strengths and weaknesses in information processing, but also in various kinds of representations of information. The test is a group test, and can be administered in its totality in three class periods. Portions of it, of course, can be administered in less.

How do the STAT test items differ from those on a conventional test? In a number of respects. For one, there is more emphasis on ability to learn than on what has been learned. For example, verbal skill is measured by learning from context, not by vocabulary (which represents products rather than processes of learning). For another, the test measures skills for coping with novelty, whereby the examinee must imagine a hypothetical state of the world (such as cats being magnetic) and then reason as though this state of the world were true. For yet another, the test measures practical abilities, such as reasoning about advertisements and political slogans, not just about decontextualized words or geometric forms. These are only a few of the differences that separate this test from its predecessors.

Do test items such as those in the STAT actually work? For one thing, many, but not all of the item types have been explored in my research on the Triarchic Theory of Human Intelligence, and only items yielding favorable outcomes have been used in the test. For another, item types have been constantly revised and re-revised until they met both our theoretical and our measurement standards. The Psychological Corporation has just completed pilot testings of the various item types, with very favorable results.

The STAT is not immune to effects of prior learning, nor is it "culture-free." It is impossible, I believe, to create a test that is genuinely immune to effects of prior experience or that is culture-free, because intelligence cannot be tested outside the boundaries of a culture. Intelligence is always used in some context, and must be measured in some context. The proposed test, however, seems broader and more comprehensive than other existing tests, and hence allows for more diversity in backgrounds than would be true of typical tests.

Through the STAT, it will be possible to extend the testing of intelligence substantially beyond the conventional boundaries. It will be possible to identify children who are gifted in unconventional ways, or who would appear mentally retarded by a conventional test but not by this one, which considers practical as well as academic intellectual skills. If we want to measure intelligence, we can and should measure it broadly rather than in the narrow ways that have failed to give a true picture of human capacities.

Mihaly Csikszentmihalyi

When the experience of learning becomes its own reward, that's being in the "flow!" Perhaps when students are challenged in ways that make it possible for them to learn—taking into consideration their ability, learning style, kinds of intelligence— and in ways that are strongly motivating, more students may reach that enviable state that Dr. Mihaly Cskiszentmihalyi so eloquently describes. His work is devoted to examining the state of "flow," how it comes about, and how it can be facilitated.

Dr. Csikszentmihalyi is professor of Human Development and Education at the University of Chicago, where he was formerly chairman of the Department of Psychology and Chairman of Human Development. After graduating and receiving his Ph.D. from the University of Chicago, he began his career as associate professor and chairman of the Department of Sociology and Anthropology at Lake Forest College. He has been a visiting professor at the University of Maine, and also at universities in Finland, Brazil, Canada, and Italy.

He currently serves on the Child Labor Advisory Committee of the United States Department of Labor and the Center for Giftedness of the federal Department of Education.

Dr. Csikszentmihalyi has published over 120 articles or chapters and eight books. The first one, *Beyond Boredom and Anxiety* (1975), went through five editions, is still in print, and has been translated into German and Japanese. The most recent book, *Flow: The Psychology of Optimal Experience*, has been selected by four book clubs, and is being translated into Danish, German, and Italian. He has also written short stories for the *New Yorker*, essays for the *Atlantic Monthly*, book reviews for the *New York Times*, and has translated fiction and poetry into English from Italian, French, and Hungarian.

THOUGHTS ABOUT EDUCATION   Mihaly Csikszentmihalyi, Ph.D.

It has turned out that mass education is more difficult to achieve than we had anticipated. To close the gap between the rather dismal reality and earlier expectations, researchers and practitioners have placed their faith in teaching methods modeled on computers and other rational means for conveying information – which in turn were modeled on industrial production techniques and on military human systems design. The implicit hope has been that if we discover more and more rational ways of selecting, organizing, and distributing knowledge, children will learn more effectively.

Yet it seems increasingly clear that the chief impediments to learning are not cognitive in nature. It is not that students cannot learn, it is that they do not wish to. Computers do not suffer from motivational problems, whereas human beings do. We have not found ways to program children so that they will learn the information we present to them as computers do. Unfortunately, cognitive science has not taken adequate notice of this fact, and hence the current cognitive emphasis on teaching is missing out on an essential component of what learning is about.

Of the two main forms of motivation—extrinsic and intrinsic—I focus pri-marily on the second kind. Although both are needed to induce people to invest energy in learning, intrinsic motivation, which is operative when we learn something primarily because we find the task enjoyable and not because it is useful, is a more effective and more satisfying way to learn.

The claim is that if educators invested a fraction of the energy on stimulating the students' enjoyment of learning that they now spend in trying to transmit information we could achieve much better results. Literacy, numeracy, or indeed any other subject matter will be mastered more readily and more thoroughly when the student becomes able to derive intrinsic rewards from learning. At present, however, lamentably few students would recognize the idea that learning can be enjoyable.

When people enjoy whatever they are doing, they report some characteristic experiential states that distinguish the enjoyable moment from the rest of life. The same dimensions are reported in the context of enjoying chess, climbing mountains, playing with babies, reading a book, or writing a poem. They are the same for young and old, male and female, American or Japanese, rich or poor. In other words, the phenomenology of enjoyment seems to be a panhuman constant. When all the characteristics are present, we call this state of consciousness a *flow experience*, because many of the respondents reported that when what they were doing was especially enjoyable it felt like being carried away by a current, like being in a flow.

A teacher who understands the conditions that make people want to learn—want to read, to write, and do sums—is in a position to turn these activities into flow experiences. When the experience becomes intrinsically rewarding, students' motivation is engaged, and they are on their way to a lifetime of self-propelled acquisition of knowledge.

Fortunately, many teachers intuitively know that the best way to achieve their goals is to enlist students' interest on their side. They do this by being sensitive to students' goals and desires, and they are thus able to articulate the pedagogical goals as meaningful challenges. They empower students to take control of their learning; they provide clear feedback to the students' efforts without threatening their egos and without making them self-conscious. They help students concentrate and get immersed in the symbolic world of the subject matter. As a result, good teachers still turn out children who enjoy learning, and who will continue to face the world with curiosity and interest.

It is to be hoped that with time the realization that children are not miniature computing machines will take root in educational circles, and more attention will be paid to motivational issues. Unless this comes to pass, the current problems we are having with education are not likely to go away.

There are two main ways that children's motivation to learn can be enhanced. The first is by a realistic reassessment of the extrinsic rewards attendant to education. This would involve a much clearer communication of the advantages and disadvantages one might expect as a result of being able to read, write, and do sums. Of course, these consequences must be real, and not just a matter of educational propaganda. Hypocrisy is easy to detect, and nothing turns motivation off more effectively than the realization that one has been had.

The second way to enhance motivation is to make children aware of how much fun learning can be. This strategy is preferable on many counts. In the first place, it is something teachers can do something about. Second, it should be easier to implement—it does not require expensive technology, although it does require sensitivity and intelligence, which might be harder to come by than the fruits of technology. Third, it is a more efficient and permanent way to empower children with the tools of knowledge. And finally, this strategy is preferable because it adds immensely to the enjoyment learners will take in the use of their abilities, and hence it improves the quality of their lives.

Noel Entwistle

Noel Entwistle is Bell Professor of Education and Director of the Centre for Research on Learning and Instruction at the University of Edinburgh.

Since 1968 his main research interested has been on student learning in higher education. He has directed a series of major studies which have contributed greatly to the understanding of how teaching and assessment affect the quality of learning.

The following description of his work seems clearly related to the previous articles on different kinds of intelligence and the characteristics of the "flow state" as he describes "deep learning" and the transformation of information into knowledge.

Professor Entwistle has been editor of the *British Journal of Education Psychology*, and currently serves on the Editorial Boards of the journals *Medical Education* and the *European Journal of the Psychology of Education*.

He is a Fellow of the British Psychological Society and has an Honorary Doctorate from the University of Gothenburg. He has published extensively in academic journals related to educational psychology and higher education.

His most recent books are *Styles of Learning and Teaching* (1981), *Understanding Student Learning* (1983), *Understanding Classroom Learning* (1987), and *The Experience of Learning* (1989, co-editor). He was general editor of *The Handbook of Educational Ideas and Practices* (1990).

LEARNING AND STUDYING: CONTRASTS AND INFLUENCES

Noel Entwistle, Ph.D.

What we learn depends on *how* we learn, and *why* we have to learn it. Recent research on the ways in which students in higher education tackle their day-to-day academic work has drawn attention to the need to think of learning as the outcome of a whole range of interacting factors. Of course, how well we learn depends on our intelligence—or rather the level of our various intelligences in relation to the task we have to do. It has been clear for many years that achievement in formal educational contexts also depends on effort, and on the general level of student motivation. But increasingly, research on student learning has been describing additional influences on academic learning. These influences depend, in part, on the individual characteristics of learners, and on their past experiences in education. They also depend on current experience within the courses they are taking—the quality of the teaching, and above all on the nature of the assessment procedures. We now have a set of related concepts which allow us to understand why some students do well, while others do badly.

The starting point has to be the reasons for which a student is taking a particular course. Some students enter higher education mainly for the intellectual challenge, or to prove they are capable of degree level work. They have an *academic orientation*. Others are more concerned with obtaining a qualification which will ensure a safe job. This is a *vocational orientation*. These different purposes inevitably affect not just the degree of effort they will put into the course, but also the *kind* of effort, as we shall see.

Students also come into higher education with different beliefs about what *learning* itself actually means. When adults from a range of ages and educational backgrounds are asked to explain what they understood by "learning," a series of contrasting conceptions is found which can be seen as a hierarchy, increasing in both sophistication and complexity. Adults hold very different *conceptions of learning*. It has been found that many people who have left school early see learning as just the result of building up separate bits of knowledge, like bricks in a wall. This view seems to be reinforced by traditional forms of education which test mainly the acquisition of facts, and also by quiz shows which reward the same kind of knowledge! Closely allied to this simplest conception is the idea that learning depends on memorizing what has to be learned. But to be useful, information eventually has to be applied in some way; this leads to a rather more sophisticated conception.

All these first three conceptions imply that information is presented to the learner whose job it is, when required, to *reproduce* that information in the same form as it was originally learned. This is not unreasonable when facts are being learned, but that is only one type of learning. Often we have to understand something for ourselves and that depends on a *transformation* of the knowledge presented, an ability to relate it to what is already known and to make personal sense of it. The more sophisticated conceptions stress the extent to which the learner has to be active in making sense of the material and, in the process, may change as a person.

Different Conceptions of Learning
(Adapted from Saljo, 1979, and Beaty, Dall'Alba, & Marton, 1990)

   A. Increasing one's knowledge

   B. Memorizing and reproducing   *Reproducing*
   C. Utilizing facts and procedures
   D. Developing an initial understanding   *Transforming*

   E. Transforming one's understanding
   F. Changing as a person

When students are asked to carry out an academic task, like preparing for a tutorial or writing an essay, the way in which they tackle that task depends on why they are taking the course and on what they believe learning requires of them. This means that when they think about how to tackle the task, different students actually have rather different *intentions.* And those intentions have proved to be closely related to how they go about learning, and the quality of the learning they achieve.

91

Research on this topic was carried out initially by Ference Marton and his colleagues in Gothenburg. From interviews with students who had been asked to read an academic article and to be "ready to answer questions on it afterwards", they distinguished between *deep* and *surface* "approaches to learning" which depended on the students' intention when tackling the task. Some students intended simply to spot facts likely to form questions, and then to memorize them; in other words they focused on the surface level of the text. Other students intended to understand what the author was saying, and so focused more deeply on the underlying meaning, and sought to integrate the components. The characteristics of these contrasting approaches are summarized below.

Defining features of approaches to learning
(Adapted from Marton et al., 1984, and Entwistle & Ransden, 1983)

Deep Approaches

Intention to understand material for oneself
Interacting vigorously and critically on content

Relating ideas to previous knowledge/experience
Using organizing principles to integrate ideas

Relating evidence to conclusions
Examining the logic of the argument

Surface Approach

Intention simply to reproduce parts of the content
Accepting ideas and information passively

Concentrating only on assessment requirements
Not reflecting on purpose or strategies in learning

Memorizing facts and procedures routinely
Failing to recognise guiding principles or patterns

The research of Fransson, Biggs and Entwistle, using interviews and questionnaires to indicate the relative strengths of deep and surface approaches, showed that each approach was associated with distinctive forms of motivation. A surface approach was associated with anxiety and fear of failure, and to some extent with vocational motives, while a deep approach was consistently linked with academic interest in the subject for its own sake, and with self-confidence. Although these forms of motivation are characteristics of the learner, interest and self-confidence, or boredom and anxiety, are also the products of experiences within higher education.

One result of these findings has been to suggest new ways of teaching study skills. Making students more aware of their own study methods and learning styles allows them to control their activities more consciously. Traditional approaches to study skills training have focused on specific skills, like note-taking or essay-writing, and yet students often seem not to transfer such training into everyday studying. More recent work has been designed to help students to see the purposes of the work they have to do, to consider strategies, and to monitor their success—in other words to become more meta-cognitively aware of the processes of studying. There is accumulating evidence that this method is effective in improving feelings of confidence and in increasing the levels of achievement, at least for students with the necessary initial motivation. Where motivation is initially low, however, it may be necessary to use more direct methods of training study skills.

Researchers have improved students' attainments by helping the students see that they can change their study methods in ways which will improve their academic performance and also by direct training in the thinking skills which underlie academic tasks.

Changing study habits, however, is not sufficient. It is also necessary to see how the teaching and assessment in a course affect how students learn. The importance of the deep approach to learning can be seen in other research which shows how it affects the level of understanding reached. In a recent study of first-year students taking a physics course, Prosser and Millar (1989) showed that only students who had used a deep approach to their learning changed their conception of technical material in the ways required by the lecturers. Students relying on surface approaches were left with inadequate conceptions that would create increasing problems for them as they progressed through the course.

Thus, we have to consider what forms of teaching and assessment evoke interest and, through that, a deep approach to learning and deeper levels of conceptual understanding. We also have to avoid establishing learning environments which inhibit the types of learning that are required. Our recent studies have shown that a deep approach is more common in departments whose students rate them as having *good teaching* and allowing *freedom in learning*. The students describe good teaching within lectures in terms of level, pace, structure, explanations, enthusiasm and empathy. Freedom in learning at its simplest level may mean no more than a reasonable choice of essay topics, but it extends into more innovative teaching methods which encourage greater independence and self-reliance. In contrast, departments which students rated as having a heavy workload, or as having assessment procedures emphasizing the accurate reproduction of detailed information, are each likely to induce a surface approach to learning and studying.

There is accumulating evidence that over-loaded syllabuses, particularly in the applied sciences, lead to student coping strategies that inhibit high quality learning. The effects of current assessment procedures are also worrying. Short-answer or multiple-choice tests, which are increasingly being used in higher education, seem to encourage surface approaches to learning, whereas essay-type examinations usually demand deep approaches. However, even essay questions may make very different demands on students, and so evoke contrasting responses. It may seem inevitable that questions which ask for an "explanation" will test conceptual understanding. To some extent this is true, but one of our recent studies has suggested different forms of "understanding." Students can "understand" their lecture notes, where they are based on a well-structured lecture course, without much active engagement with the ideas. They can accept the information within the lecturer's own structure and repeat it in only a slightly modified form in the examination. The explanation will generally be accepted as "sound", even if evidence of wider reading is lacking, as the structure of the answer will reflect the understanding of the lecturer. But such a reproductive argument will not represent evidence of the student's own conceptual understanding. Thus it cannot indicate whether the student will be able to apply those ideas to novel situations.

Besides teaching and assessment as separate influences, it is also clear that the approach to learning is affected by the curriculum as a whole. Putting together the accumulating evidence on the effects of learning environments on the quality of student learning, it is possible to alter courses, including the teaching and assessment procedures, in ways which more directly support a deep approach to learning.

Asa Hilliard III

In a recent article, Dr. Asa Hilliard notes that for many years he has been "fortunate enough to see first hand individual teachers and whole schools that were consistently successful in producing the highest level of academic excellence with those students who are regarded as the most likely candidates for failure." He notes that African-American, Hispanic, American Indian, and poor children can and do blossom academically and socially under the right school conditions. "These successes destroy forever the whole inventory of excuses for our failure to educate all children at the level that we now call 'excellence'."

Devoting his life to helping all children to learn, he has served on innumerable advisory boards for national, state, and community organizations focused on the education of minority students, young children, and children with special needs, as well as on boards dealing with assessment, teacher education, and mental health.

He has been director for numerous research projects, including Research on Multi-ethnic Curriculum Issues for New York College Boards, a national research project for the National Education Association on the subject of the declining numbers of black teachers, and a Toddlers and Infants Evaluation Study for Oakland, California.

At the present time, Dr. Hilliard is Fuller E. Callaway Professor of Urban Education, Department of Educational Foundations, Counselling and Psychological Services, and Early Childhood Education at Georgia State University in Atlanta, Georgia. He recently served as Editorial Consultant for John Garrity's *The Story of America*, and produced a video program, with Listervelt Middelton, *Master Keys to Ancient Kemet*.

He was given the Outstanding Scholarship Award by the National Association of Black Psychologists and the Marcus A. Foster Distinguished Educator Award by the National Alliance of Black School Educators.

CULTURAL PLURALISM IN EDUCATION   Asa Hilliard III, Ph.D.

Now and then we hear these wonderful stories about the little old lady who weighs no more than 135 pounds who finds that a large truck has fallen off a jack and is crushing her husband to death. With what appears to be miraculous strength, she moves in and actually lifts the truck, enabling the husband to be rescued. Apparently, she always had the strength; all that was needed was to focus the energies in a determined effort to succeed.

Learning ought to be like that; in fact, in many cases, it is precisely like that. For many years, I have been concerned that we do not see it this way. There is rather a brutal pessimism which permeates the expectations of too many of us; those on the front lines, and those in more remote policy positions – perhaps even those in the general public at large. We have adjusted to very low levels of performance from children in the schools; now it takes very little to satisfy us.

For the past two decades, my writing and research has been focused on pedagogical success in two areas. On the one hand, I continue to be intrigued and exhilarated by educators who are winning magnificently. That is, educators who are able to teach so that the masses of students that they teach have excellent performance. At the same time, I am fascinated and exhilarated when I have the opportunity to observe those magnificent teacher educators, who like excellent teachers, are able to transfer their knowledge of excellent teaching to raw recruits.

In spite of the changes in perception among educators that have come about because of the Effective Schools movement, I believe that we have yet to be captured by a vision of an excellent school movement. For too many, such a goal seems closer to fantasy than reality. As a result, I have tried to highlight many examples of excellence in teaching and teacher education in the hope that they would be noticed by a broad audience, and where possible, that they would be imitated. Teaching and research should begin in most instances from an examination of power teaching.

I have also been concerned about what children are taught. Of course, the way children are taught and the content of their lessons are integral to each other. The content of school course work is never neutral. It has an effect on children, one way or the other. Much of my career, I have been concerned with the problem of low performance of African-American, Hispanic-American, and American Indian students, as well as poor European students. I have had the opportunity to review many types of curricula and materials that support the curriculum. In spite of the fact that the issue of cultural pluralism in the curriculum has been raised as a problem for many years now, fundamental changes have yet to be made. When I think of pluralism in the curriculum, I think first and foremost of a truthful curriculum that paints an accurate picture of the total human experience, no matter what events we choose to examine. A truthful portrayal of human events will force a pluralization of the curriculum instantly.

Children, no matter what their racial or ethnic background, should be presented with pictures of the real world. That is how we can support accurate perception. In addition, this is how we assure that children from every group will find themselves at the center of materials that they study. Motivation and self-esteem are deeply affected by the topics that we choose to present and by the coverage we choose to give those topics from a pluralistic perspective. As it is true that there are many models of teaching that result in excellence in student achievement, there are also many models of excellence in pluralistic curriculum. However, as with pedagogical success, curricular success tends to be out of the awareness of the majority of our educators.

Educational reform must address these two issues. The "miracle" that I cited at the beginning of this article has its counterpart in education. Excellent performance by students and excellence in the curriculum is not a matter of miracles, however; it only appears to be so. There are many living examples of the fact that hard work and clear focus can transform the educational condition of our students, and even the condition of educators that serve them.

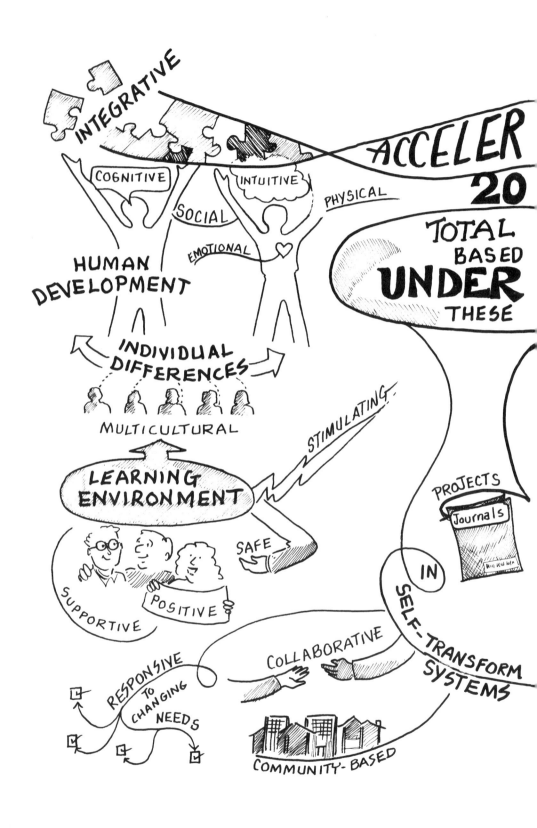

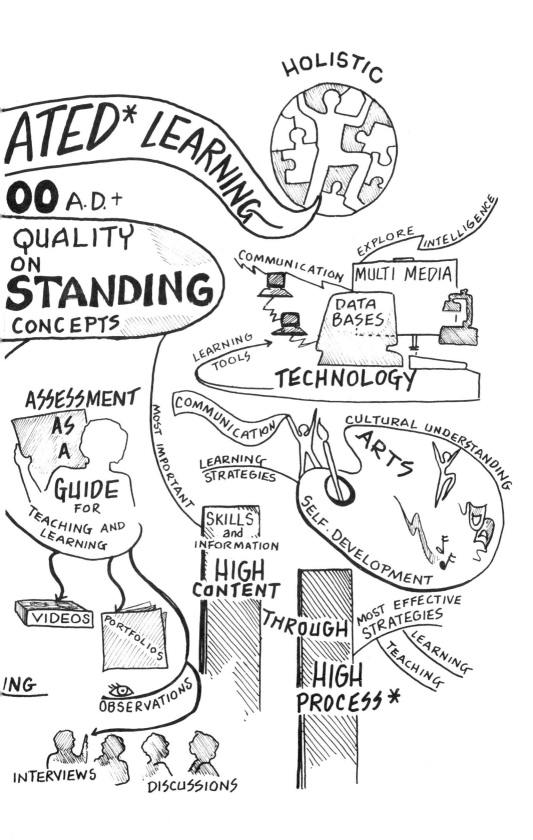

Paul Messier

Dr. Paul Messier is Senior Research Analyst for the United States Department of Education and Director of the Quality Mentoring Project for the One to One Program. His commitment to education has been of long standing as a teacher on all levels, Fulbright Scholar, researcher, and now, with his current interests in gathering the most effective and innovative strategies for teaching and learning, as director of the White House Task Force on Innovative Learning.

During the Education Summit on Lifespan Learning, Dr. Messier presented his "Education Bill of Rights" for the 21st Century. In it he describes the need to "identify and applaud schools that work, methods that work, and models that work—and work in ways that transcend traditional modes—that work by doing more than disseminating knowledge and skills, that develop self-starting, self-confident, self-actualizing individuals who know how to learn and also how to thrive on learning.... Models are needed to engage broader human capabilities and achieve massive enhancements of education, enhancements that alter our fundamental perceptions of learning and learners."

After graduating from Lowell University, Dr. Messier attended Columbia University, where he received a master's degree in Counseling Psychology. He received his Education Certificate from San Diego University, and his Ph.D. in Social Psychology from Michigan State University, followed by postdoctoral research as a Fulbright Scholar in Florence and at George Washington University.

Dr. Messier entered the United States Office of Education as a Research Specialist in 1963. He has served as Associate Director of Research and Development for Project Head Start. In the US Department of Education he has served as Director of Regional Research and Development, Associate Deputy Commissioner, Director of the Division of Development, Director of Special Studies, and Acting Director of the Education and Society Division, Office of Research, Office of Educational Research and Improvement.

For much of my research career, I sought "objective" data so as to be on firm ground and avoided "subjective" influences on my observations. The more "objective" the observation, the more solidly it approached the real truth. This is such a fundamental "given" in research that the assumption is held without question and tacitly guides inquiry. Of course, being "objective" makes the observation verifiable by another observer. This is the strength of the scientific method. When Isaac Newton ushered in the age of science, he gave us a new paradigm; a new way of exploring. But to become scientific, we had to prevent our views from intruding on facts. The

103

wonders of science became ours only as we became uninvolved observers. We then set about finding the truths in nature and exposed them for others to witness.

This is all very understandable to me and represents progress in knowing facts ever more clearly. Moreover, it simply feels right—an "objective" fact is more real than a "subjective" one. The biases inherent in a "subjective" fact obviously distort the truth.

To refine our facts further E. L. Thorndike observed that (1) if something exists, it exists in some amount, and (2) to know something well involves knowing its quantity. These straightforward pronouncements lay down a credo for research. The better you can measure it, the more real it is! Put another way, if it can't be measured, it probably doesn't exist. With measurements, the verification of a fact can become very precise. When your measurements match mine, then we know we are observing the same objective reality.

Measuring subjective judgments is an annoyingly inaccurate, if not an impossible, job. To share a subjective observation with some degree of precision is virtually unattainable. It does appear that subjective observations lack something necessary to make them tangible. You can't confirm that you're seeing the same thing that I am. At the very least, subjective observations should be relegated to a lesser realm of reality—and that feels all right. It fits the way things are. For example, we have the "hard" physical sciences and the "soft" social sciences. We know that physics is the stalwart of the exact sciences, while psychology is still trying to measure things accurately.

This all seems to be natural and proper. It is how reality has been worked out. Moreover, it agrees very well with the world as we know it. Or could it be something about us that would have us see the world this way? If so, how did we get "this way" of seeing? Is it in our genetic design? Or, perhaps, it comes from the common

way we have of viewing things—our way of viewing the world—
our world view?

The answer literally came home to me as I was helping my six-
year-old daughter, Rachel, prepare balloons for her birthday party.
I tied a string on a balloon, held the string out taut and asked her to
cut it with the scissors. As she picked up the scissors she asked me
where she should cut the string. I told her that anywhere would do
the job. She held the scissors over the string and asked if where she
had placed the scissors would do. As I attended to other things, I
replied that anywhere around the middle would be fine. Then my
attention focused on her as she moved the scissors back and forth
across the middle of the string. With anxious concentration, she
brought the scissors to rest in one position and asked if that were the
center. I told her it was and she proceeded to cut the string.

I was concerned with what I had just observed. Rachel is in the
first grade and is identified as gifted. She had always exhibited a
great deal of confidence in herself. But it became clear to me that she
was becoming doubtful about her own judgment. Assurance as to
where the "center" was had to come from me. Certainly, if Rachel
had been in school she would have asked the teacher to specify the
"center." The teacher, in turn, would have seen this as very
appropriate and Rachel would be rewarded for being careful and
thoughtful about following directions.

Rachel had just begun her schooling and was already becoming
aware about the fundamental "nature-of-things." She was beginning
to understand that the truth—the exact location of the "center"—
resided outside of herself. The truth was to be found in persons of
authority or out there somewhere in the reality of things. If she
asked and searched hard enough and long enough she would know
the "center" of things. The world that she knew, the one that
resided within herself, the one she put together from her own sense
of things was to be set aside. The world wherein her own "center"

resides was becoming suspect. The quest for the remainder of her life was being clearly set before her: to seek out the truths that reside "out there."

The rules of the quest will soon come to feel natural. And as she conducts her research in graduate school, she will intrinsically know that "objective" data are more solid than "subjective" data. She will know what the researcher of today knows, that "subjective" biases are to be avoided if the real truth is to be known. And this will all be understandable and feel right!

On the other hand, this scenario should perhaps be reconsidered. These are times of change, and it appears our reality is changing. At least, our view of reality is changing and "our view" apparently has something to do with the changes. The tenets of Newtonian physics, where the firmest of "objective" facts have been found over these many years, may not stand on solid ground as it turns out. The new physics is convinced that separating the "observer" from the "observed" is quite impossible. How then can we step back and observe "objectively"? Perhaps unbiased observation is a sham, for the act of observing itself alters what we are observing.

Moreover, according to the new physics, how you set about measuring something determines what you will measure. Whatever you set out to measure is what you'll get. So, even measurements can't firm up "objective" reality for us, for the act of measuring itself delimits what is being measured. Our "subjective" world impinges on the "objective" world.

The goal of grasping "objective" reality is further removed as the complex wonders of chaos are unfolded. Chaos, nonlinear dynamics, is now recognized as being the rule rather than the exception throughout nature and the universe. The old rules that gave us an orderly, repeating "reality" were comfortable, but unfortunately inaccurate. To gain this appealing regularity, we unwittingly shape reality to our liking. We allow our need for neat, straightforward patterns to govern what facts we accept as important. These straight-line, linear patterns enable us to make predictions.

Comforting, yes, but what of the facts that do not fit the patterns we wanted? To keep things tidy, they are declared inconsequential and are dismissed as insignificant. Not fitting our paradigm, we're sometimes not even aware of them, as Thomas Kuhn pointed out. They do not disappear, however. The studies of chaos have taken another look at them. These discarded or overlooked facts now reveal themselves as key to producing chaotic, nonlinear patterns—nature's preeminent design—beautiful, irregular patterns, but not comfortably predictable.

So, it turns out, we've been tailoring our discoveries of "objective" realities to suit our predilections—to fit our composite "subjective" reality—to conform to our paradigm. Perhaps, in fact, reality is neither "objective" nor "subjective." Together they comprise the reality we know and both are equally important in its composition. What we subjectively put in is as important as the objective component—subjective and objective are equally important.

Maybe Rachel and her teacher shouldn't try to replace her world with an "objective" one. Maybe it's time to render a new judgment on the primacy of the "objective" world. It comprises but part of our reality with our "subjective" view providing the remainder. Our socially agreed upon "subjective" view, our way of seeing things, our paradigm as it relates to our individual worlds is important to understand. In turn, it would seem important to know our individual worlds as they impact on our reality. Accordingly, Rachel should be encouraged to develop and understand her own world. Her unique world and that of all students should be cherished for the enrichment they offer our reality. These young worlds should be nurtured with care and dignity for they, in composite, will shape the reality of tomorrow.

Robert McClure

Dr. Robert McClure is director of the National Education Association's site-based restructuring program of the Center for Innovation. Formerly he was director of the NEA's Mastery In Learning Project, a five-year national research and development effort in which knowledge about teaching, learning, and curriculum was used by faculties to improve their schools.

Dr. McClure's dedication to improving the quality of education nationwide is evident in his long-standing efforts in the field. He joined the NEA Center for the Study of Instruction in 1964 to help create the Schools for the Seventies program, and in 1975 developed a federally funded research utilization program which led to the inservice education programs of the Regional Educational Laboratories. A seventeen-volume report is still used as a reference guide to those programs.

As a champion for enhancing the role of teachers as key decision-makers in education, he has written and spoken widely, and he serves as editor of the new *School Restructuring Series* of the NEA Professional Library. *Teachers and Researchers in Action*, the first book in the series, is being used throughout the country in teaching and research communities. He edited the Seventieth Yearbook of the National Society of Education, *The Curriculum: Retrospect and Prospect*, and has written chapters for more than a dozen other books.

Dr. McClure received his master's degree in Curriculum Development and School Administration from the University of Southern California, and his doctorate in Curriculum and Social Psychology from UCLA. In the mid-seventies he was Distinguished Scholar at the Far West Laboratory for Educational Research and Development.

EDUCATIONAL RESTRUCTURING   Robert McClure, Ph.D.

There was very little involvement of teachers or other practitioners in the several commissions that shaped the effort to renew schools in the early 1980's. In an attempt to bring the voices of teachers to the national discussion, Mary Hatwood Futrell, President of the National Education Association, in 1983 appointed a commission to make recommendations about the future of schooling. Comprised of twenty classroom teachers from across the country, the task force produced *An Open Letter to America About Schools, Students, and Tomorrow* (National Education Association,

1984). Using that report as a springboard, the Mastery In Learning Project began in the spring of 1985.

The focus of the project is on the essentials of schooling—learning, curriculum, teaching—and how these interrelate to define the culture or climate of the school. The resources of the Project are used to enable the faculty to create the conditions necessary for students to master important knowledge and skills. MIL asks the faculty and its community to recreate their school to reflect:

☐ The best that is known about teaching, learning, curriculum, and school climate;

☐ The faculty's and community's best aspirations for its students.

In other words, the project did not predetermine what schools should be like as a result of reformation and then set out to achieve that vision. Rather, it set out to test the idea that school faculties which had access to current knowledge, research, and exemplars of good practice could, given the authority, "grow a school" that would better serve its students than one reformed by outside mandates. Many school renewal efforts, particularly those initiated by state legislatures and governors' offices, had relied on a mandated, top-down approach to improvement.

To demonstrate to policy makers and others the efficacy of another approach, MIL created in 1986 a demographically representative network of twenty-six schools. As a group, the schools in the network are representative of all schools in the country regarding socioeconomic levels, ethnicity, race, type of community, and nature of the organization of the school.

As the teachers and administrators talked about curriculum, teaching, learning, and school climate at the outset of the Project, several findings emerged:

☐ Principals and teachers relied heavily on textbook manuals, mandates from outside the school, directives from supervisors, and advice from others in similar roles. They accepted the status quo and doubted that challenges to it would have much impact.

☐ Most of the practitioners in the network knew about or had experienced previous efforts to improve schools and believed that much of that work had been misguided and done more harm than good. They believed that it was their responsibility to resist efforts that would, once again, do damage to educational quality.

☐ Most staff members did not describe themselves as risk takers. They saw their school system as closed organizations uninterested in input from "low level" staff, organizations that punished those who took risks.

☐ School staffs accepted, almost unquestioningly, the technologies that control schooling: behavioral objectives, textbooks, and standardized tests.

When asked to select words that described their school, the following were often used: *memory, textbooks, uniform, classrooms, separate subjects, broad curriculum, student testing that stresses recall, central decision making, teacher burnout.*

Although the local faculty (defined as teachers, administrators, and others that held the school responsible for the educational program) now design the reform agenda, the Project provides the processes by which their restructuring would occur:

☐ *Phase One:* PROFILING THE SCHOOL (several weeks). Through structured interviews with teachers, students, parents, and administrators, a description of the school is created to serve as a benchmark for the Project's efforts.

☐ *Phase Two:* INVENTORYING THE FACULTY (several days). Through a process that reveals similarities and differences in priorities and aspirations among faculty members, the school faculty establishes initial priorities for improvement.

☐ *Phase Three:* FACULTY ENABLEMENT (two to three years). The faculty works to create the skills, attitudes, and inclinations necessary for sustained inquiry into the assumptions and practices that define their school.

☐ *Phase Four:* COMPREHENSIVE CHANGE (ongoing). Having developed skills and habits of collaboration and collegiality and a clearer vision of what is desirable for their school with regard to learning, teaching, curriculum, and school climate, the faculty engages in ongoing systemic school improvement.

For the most part, faculties in the network schools are different now from the way they were at the outset of the Project. They are increasingly aware of the knowledge base that undergirds their work and are more likely to consider it useful in solving their problems.

They see themselves as powerful shapers of the future of their school; are more collegial and less isolated; more savvy about the politics of school systems; better able to view their school in a comprehensive manner. They think they can be influential in affecting student learning. They are more passionate about the values they hold.

Charles Thompson, who examined reports of several MIL faculties' efforts to improve their educational program, commented on the enabling, empowering aspect of this work:

> These revolutions are not, however, simple redistributions of power. These revolutions multiply it. New knowledge . . . emboldens teachers to think, to examine their practice. And there is an almost electric sense of energy release that accompanies this realization, a sense of excitement that raises the energy level throughout each building.

Faculty-led school improvement efforts that are context-specific, student outcome-oriented, intellectually valid, and professionally enabling offer a significant opportunity to make fundamental improvement in America's schools.

Malcolm S. Knowles

Dr. Malcolm Knowles concludes his book *Andragogy in Action* by noting that "We are nearing the end of the era of our edifice complex and its basic belief that respectable learning takes place only in buildings and on campuses. Adults are beginning to demand that their learning take place at a time, place, and pace convenient to them. In fact, I feel confident that most educational services by the end of this century (if not decade) will be delivered electronically . . . . Our great challenge now is to find ways to maintain the human touch as we learn to use the media in new ways."

His quest for finding these new ways has led to his development of a self-directed, andragogical model of learning and of the conception of community learning centers as new kinds of educational facilities where lifelong learning can take place. Indeed intergenerational learning is a common element in many of the programs where his dreams are materializing, and which are encouraging self-directed learning at all ages.

In 1960 he developed a new graduate program in adult education at Boston University, and during the next fourteen years he applied the principles of adult learning in his laboratory. He put much of what developed in his 1970 book *The Modern Practice of Adult Education: Andragogy Versus Pedagogy.*

Dr. Knowles is Professor Emeritus of Adult and Community College Education at North Carolina State University. Since his retirement from North Carolina State University in 1979, he has been an active consultant to business and industry, government agencies, educational institutions, religious institutions, and volunteer groups throughout the world.

LIFELONG LEARNING: A DREAM   Malcolm Knowles, Ph.D.

There is a dream I have had for a long time—a lifelong learning center in every community. I just dreamed it once again. The calendar on my bedroom wall showed that it was January 1, 2001 A.D., and the surroundings in my dream place me in Anyplace, U.S.A. (Later dreams put me down in villages and cities all over the world.)

I saw people of all ages going into and coming out of the center, which had lettering over its door: "Main Street Lifelong Learning Center." This suggested to me that there were similar centers in other parts of the town—perhaps within walking distance of every

115

citizen. I joined a family group consisting of a four-year-old boy, a fourteen-year-old girl, a mother and father in their mid-thirties, and a grandmother in her late sixties, and I entered with them.

We were greeted by a receptionist who referred each individual to a small office in a wing of the building labeled "Learning Skill Assessment Laboratory." I chose to accompany (invisibly) the four-year-old boy. When he entered the little office he was greeted by a charming young lady who invited him to sit by her and she explained that the purpose of their meeting was to help him get ready to take charge of his own learning with the support of the staff of the Center. She gave him a few assessment exercises designed to determine the levels of his skills in planning and carrying out learning projects and gave him a form showing his ratings on eight skill dimensions (his "Learning Skill Profile"). She congratulated him on having achieved the appropriate level of skill for four-year-olds in all dimensions, and referred him to a helper who served as educational diagnostician in another office down the hall.

While we were waiting in the lounge area for an educational diagnostician to become available I was able to check out with the other members of the family what their experience had been and learned that each of them showed some weakness in one or two learning skills and had been given corrective exercises to work on at home. They were given the following learning skills inventory:

SKILLS OF SELF-DIRECTED LEARNING

1. The ability to develop and be in touch with curiosities. Perhaps another way to describe this skill would be "the ability to engage in divergent thinking."

2. The ability to perceive one's self objectively and accept feedback about one's performance nondefensively.

3. The ability to diagnose one's learning needs in the light of models of competencies required for performing life roles.

4. The ability to formulate learning objectives in terms that describe performance outcomes.

5. The ability to identify human, material, and experiential resources for accomplishing various kinds of learning objectives.

6. The ability to design a plan of strategies for making use of appropriate learning resources effectively.

7. The ability to carry out a learning plan systematically and sequentially. This skill is the beginning of the ability to engage in convergent thinking.

8. The ability to collect evidence of the accomplishment of learning objectives and have it validated through performance.

The educational diagnostician, another charming young lady, greeted our four-year-old boy warmly and started asking him questions about what he would like to be able to do when he was five years old. I could see that she was being guided in her questioning by a list of "competencies for performing life roles" lying on her desk (and reprinted here). As she talked with him it became clear that he had aspirations "to get ready for school," to "get along better with the kids," and to "have a little more fun." She then gave him a few simple exercises to perform to assess his level of knowledge and skill for performing the roles of learner, friend, and leisure-time user. She noted the results of the exercises on a form and gave it to him to take to the next helper, an educational planning consultant, in another wing of the building.

117

While we were waiting in the lounge area I had a chance to check out with the other family members what had happened to them. The fourteen-year-old girl had identified some competencies for the role of learner (i.e. being a self, friend, citizen, and family member) that she wanted to work on. The mother was most concerned with improving her competencies in the role of family member, worker, and leisure-time user; the father, in the roles of worker and leisure-time user; and the grandmother, in the roles of learner (she felt that she had sort of "stagnated" in this regard) and leisure-time user (she wanted to learn to play the piano).

COMPETENCIES FOR PERFORMING LIFE ROLES

ROLES	COMPETENCIES
Learner	Reading, writing, computing, perceiving, conceptualizing, imagining, inquiring, aspiring, diagnosing, planning, getting help, evaluating.
Being a self (with a unique self-identity)	Self-analyzing, sensing, goal-building, objectivizing, value-clarifying, expressing, accepting, being authentic.
Friend	Loving, empathizing, listening, collaborating, sharing, helping, giving constructive feedback, supporting.
Citizen	Caring, participating, leading, decisionmaking, acting, being sensitive to one's conscience, discussing, having perspective (historical and cultural), being a global citizen.

Family Member   Maintaining health, planning, managing, help-
                     ing, sharing, buying, saving, loving, taking re-
                     sponsibility.

Worker   Career planning, using technical skills, accept-
                     ing supervision, giving supervision, getting
                     along with people, cooperating, planning, del-
                     egating, managing.

Leisure-time user   Knowing resources, appreciating the arts and
                     humanities, performing, playing, relaxing,
                     reflecting, planning, risking.

I accompanied our four-year-old boy into the office of the educational consultant, who gave me the impression of being a kindly retired school teacher. After some get-acquainted talk with the boy, he looked at the forms filled out by the learning skills assessor and the educational diagnostician. After further discussion it was agreed that the learning project the boy would like to start with was "getting ready for school" and that his first objective was "Finding out what school is like." The consultant pulled a form headed "Learning Plan" from his desk and they began filling it out together. The form had five columns, the first one headed "What Are You Going to Learn?" (Learning Objectives), in which they wrote "To find out what school is like." The second column was headed "How Are You Going To Learn It?" (Resources and Strategies), and in this one they wrote "Talk to three first graders and three kindergartners"; "Visit Miss Smith's first grade class for two days," (which the consultant arranged); and "Have my sister read *Johnny Starts to School* to me" (a copy of which the consultant gave the boy). The third column, headed "Target Date," had the notation "Christmas." The fourth column, headed "Evidence of

119

Accomplishment", had the notation, "Give an oral report (tell) to my sister, mother, father, and grandmother." The fifth column, headed "Verification of Evidence," had the notation, "They agree that I have the picture." The consultant thanked the boy for his cooperation and gave him a card with the date on it for a return visit after Christmas to plan his next learning project.

I met the rest of the family in the lounge area and they proudly showed me their learning plans. The sister's plan called for her to strengthen her interpersonal relations skills, and she was scheduled to enroll in a teen-age human relations training group at the Y.W.C.A. for three months. The mother's plan called for her to start learning about career planning by participating in a career-planning workshop at the community college. The father's plan had as its first objective, "To develop knowledge and skill in computer programming," and he was to be linked up with a volunteer tutor who was a member of a local computer networking group. And, sure enough, the grandmother had been enrolled in a beginners' piano class at the local conservatory.

When I awoke from this dream I realized that my personal dream-giver had graced me with a bare snapshot of a vision of a transformative model of education for the future—a conceptualization of a community as a system of learning resources; truly, a learning community in which continuing learning throughout life is a basic organizing principle for the whole enterprise. As I let my mind wander I could visualize a community in which every individual, every organization, and every institution was perceived as a resource for learning.

I could visualize this system of resources being managed by a coordinating body representative of the various categories of individuals, organizations, and institutions. But the heart of this system—the entity that made it work—was the network of community learning centers. They were the depositories of information about all of the learning resources in the community (in electronic data banks). They housed the specialists—learning skills assessors, educational diagnosticians, educational planning consultants—and support staffs that linked all citizens of the community of all ages to appropriate learning resources and gave them the skills and support necessary to use them effectively for lifelong learning.

This dream that I have had for so long is becoming a reality as new kinds of community learning centers are being developed in every part of our country and other countries as well. These are the new forms of education that are emerging from a society in the process of transformation. They are themselves "learning systems" that are capable of bringing about their own continuing transformation—truly responsive to a learning society!

Charles Fowler

In his book *Can We Rescue the Arts for America's Children?* Dr. Charles Fowler says, "The arts are not just important; they are a central force in human existence. Each citizen should have sufficient and equal opportunities to learn these languages, which so assist us in our fumbling, bumbling, and all-too-rarely brilliant navigation through this world. Because of this, the arts should be granted major status in American schooling. That is a cause worthy of our energies."

As a practitioner of several arts with a background of teaching on every level, Dr. Fowler is an eloquent spokesman on behalf of the arts in education. He has lectured and consulted extensively on this topic throughout the United States and abroad, and has written more than two hundred articles, as well as numerous books and reports. For fifteen years he served as Education Editor of *Musical America* magazine, and was also editor of *Music Educators' Journal*. Among his recent publications is *Sing!*, a new textbook for secondary school choral classes. He is currently director of National Cultural Resources Inc. in Washington, D.C.

Dr. Fowler received a Master of Music degree from Northwestern University and a Doctor of Musical Arts degree from Boston University. He has written educational materials for the New York Philharmonic, the Metropolitan Opera, the National Endowment for the Arts, and the John F. Kennedy Center for the Performing Arts.

He was the script writer for the grand opening of the Epcot Center for Walt Disney Productions, for the grand opening of Knoxville World's Fair, and he has written scripts for a number of music programs on National Public Radio. He has prepared scripts for José Ferrar, Richard Thomas, Gregory Peck, President Gerald Ford, and Dinah Shore, among others.

EVERY CHILD NEEDS THE ARTS   Charles Fowler, D.M.A.

The arts are windows on the world in the same way that science helps us see the world around us. Literature, music, theater, the visual arts, the media (film, photography, and television), architecture, and dance reveal aspects about ourselves, the world around us, and the relationship between the two. In 1937, German planes flying for Franco in the Spanish civil war bombed a defenseless village as a laboratory experiment, killing many of the inhabitants. In *Guernica*, Pablo Picasso painted his outrage in the form of a vicious bull smugly surveying a scene of human beings screaming,

123

suffering, and dying. These powerful images etch in our minds the horror of a senseless act of war.

Similar themes have been represented in other art forms. Benjamin Britten's *War Requiem* gives poignant musical and poetic expression to the unpredictable misfortunes of war's carnage. Britten juxtaposes the verses of Wilfred Owen, a poet killed during World War I, with the ancient scriptures of the Mass for the Dead. In Euripides' play *The Trojan Women*, the ancient art of theater expresses the grievous sacrifices that war forces human beings to endure. The film *Platoon*, written and directed by Oliver Stone, is a more recent exposition of the *meaning* of war, a theme that has been treated again and again with telling effect in literature throughout the ages. The theme of human beings inflicting suffering upon other human beings has also been expressed through dance. One example is *Dreams*, a modern dance choreographed by Anna Sokolow, in which the dreams become nightmares of Nazi concentration camps.

This theme and many others are investigated, expressed, and communicated through the arts. Through such artistic representations, we share a common humanity. What would life be without such shared expressions? How would such understandings be conveyed? Science is not the sole conveyor of truth. While science can explain a sunrise, the arts convey its emotive impact and meaning. Both are important. If human beings are to survive, we need all the symbolic forms at our command because they permit us not only to preserve and pass along our accumulated wisdom but also to give voice to the invention of new visions. We need all these ways of viewing the world because no one way can say it all.

The arts are *acts of intelligence* no less than other subjects. They are forms of thought every bit as potent as mathematical and scientific symbols in what they convey. The Egyptian pyramids can be "described" in mathematical measurements, and science and history can hypothesize about how, why, and when they were built, but a photograph or painting of them can show us other equally important aspects of their reality. The arts are symbol systems that permit us to give representation to our ideas, concepts, and feelings in a variety of forms that can be "read" by other people. The arts were invented to enable us to react to the world, to analyze it, and to record our impressions so that they can be shared. Like other symbol systems, the arts require study before they can be fully understood.

Is there a better way to gain an understanding of ancient Greek civilization than through their magnificent temples, statues, pottery, and poetry? The Gothic cathedrals inform us about the Middle Ages just as surely as the skyscraper reveals the Modern Age. The arts may well be the most telling imprints of any civilization. In this sense they are living histories of eras and peoples, and records and revelations of the human spirit. One might well ask how history could possibly be taught without their inclusion.

Today's schools are concerned, as they rightly should be, with teaching literacy. But literacy should not–must not–be limited to the written word. It should also encompass the symbol systems of the arts. If our concept of literacy is defined too narrowly as referring to just the symbol systems of language, mathematics, and science, children will not be equipped with the breadth of symbolic tools they need to fully represent, express, and communicate the full spectrum of human life.

What constitutes a good education anyway? Today, one major goal has become very practical: employability. Children should know how to read, write, and compute so that they can assume a place in the work force. Few would argue with that. Considering the demands that young people will face tomorrow in this technological society, the need for literacy in English language, mathematics, science, and history is critical. But this objective should not allow us to overlook the importance of the arts and what they can do for the mind and spirit of every child and the vitality of American schooling.

Educational administrators and school boards need to be reminded that schools have a fundamental obligation to provide the fuel that will ignite the mind, spark the aspirations, and illuminate the total being. The arts can often serve as that fuel. They are the ways we apply our imagination, thought, and feeling through a range of "languages" to illuminate life in all its mystery, misery, delight, pity, and wonder. They are fundamental enablers that can help us engage more significantly with our inner selves and the world around us. As we first engage one capacity, we enable others, too, to emerge. Given the current dropout rate, whether the entry vehicle to learning for a particular human being happens to be the arts, the sciences, or the humanities is less important than the assured existence of a variety of such vehicles.

The first wave of the education reform movement in America focused on improving the quality of public education simply by raising standards and introducing more challenging course requirements at the high school level. The second wave has focused on improving the quality of the nation's teachers. The third wave should concentrate on the students–how to activate and inspire them, how to induce self-discipline, and how to help them to discover the joys of learning, the uniqueness of their beings, the wonders and possibilities of life, the satisfaction of achievement, and the revelations that literacy, broadly defined, provides. The arts are a central and fundamental means to attain these objectives.

We do not need more and better arts education simply to develop more and better artists. There are far more important reasons for schools to provide children with an education in the arts. Quite simply, the arts are the ways we human beings "talk" to ourselves and to each other. They are the language of civilization through which we express our fears, our anxieties, our curiosities, our hungers, our discoveries, and our hopes. They are the universal ways by which we humans still play make-believe, conjuring up worlds that explain the ceremonies of our lives. The arts are not just important; they are a central force in human existence. Every child should have sufficient opportunity to acquire familiarity with these languages that so assist us in our fumbling, bumbling, and all-too-rarely brilliant navigation through this world. Because of this, the arts should be granted major status in every child's schooling.

Colin Rose

Colin Rose is motivated by a clear thought. An economist by training, and an honors graduate of the London School of Economics, he sees society's biggest asset as the educational standard and creativity of its people. Yet we fail to invest enough in that asset.

Personal conviction led him in 1985 to research, write, and publish a book called *Accelerated Learning*. It was an attempted synthesis of the then new directions in teaching and learning. Public reaction to the book convinced him to found a publishing company— Accelerated Systems Ltd. Its aim is to establish contacts with those researchers and practitioners in education and training who have answers to the question, "How do I begin to realize my potential?" Colin Rose is committed to seeing that their ideas reach the widest possible audience.

He sees the contribution of Accelerated Learning Systems as publishing courses and programs that present subjects in new ways that actually do accommodate a wide range of learning styles and preferences. "Vision has to be turned into reality."

Colin Rose's grass roots approach to change has meant that he is a frequent speaker at international training and educational conferences.

His company is currently consulting with national educational authorities and international corporations and has just completed a Learn-to-Learn program for 44,000 employees of one of Britain's biggest industrial companies.

BREAKING FREE OF LIMITATIONS

The challenges and opportunities that face us today are significant. The velocity of change is accelerating. Knowledge, measured by the output of scientific papers, is doubling every two to three years, and people must now contemplate not "a" career, but three or four in their lifetime.

Industrialized countries cannot compete internationally on labor costs. To maintain and improve on living standards they must compete on skill, quality and innovation. Moreover, the Information Age has changed the emphasis on what learning means. Storage and retrieval of data can be done more efficiently by computers. We need to teach people to do what computers cannot. The premium is on creativity, problem solving, team work and self reliance.

All this requires a high level of post-compulsory education and training. Yet most people see education as something they finished when they left school. They limit themselves by a low (albeit incorrect), expectation of their ability to learn. and have little wish to return.

One study has shown that over 80% of children at age six have a high confidence in their ability to learn. That drops to 18% at age sixteen. When people feel inadequate to achieve long-term goals, they frequently settle for short-term gratifications and uncooperative behavior born of frustration. They waste their potential.

The answers, of course, are complex. However, there is one answer that seems very clear. When the only constant is change, teaching people **how** to learn must surely be a logical initial priority over **what** they learn. What you learn can become outdated. How to learn is a skill for life.

A SIX-STAGE MODEL OF LEARNING

There are two parties in any learning situation: the learner and the teacher—that includes not just the classroom teacher, but also the textwriter, TV director, or audio tape producer. If both parties had the same clear model of how to produce an effective learning situation, teaching styles and learning styles would start to match, and you would have the basis for what we call Accelerated Learning.

Drawing heavily upon the pioneering work of many of the contributors to this book, as well as Georgi Lozanov, I would like to put forward such a model of learning. It is not intended to be definitive, and no doubt it will be modified over time. What it does do, however, is act as a simple, easily understood framework for both the learner and the instructor.

Our contention is that there are six specific stages in an effective learning situation:

1.   State of Mind

The learners' states of mind determine how well they will do. They need to be made aware that their capacity to learn is very substantial at any age. So tell them how the brain works.

Tell them about Marian Diamond's work—that the brain literally expands with use. Tell them about the work of David Perkins, Robert Sternberg and others, that suggests you learn to be intelligent. I.Q., if it is anything at all, is not fixed.

The learners need to see the relevance of the learning task to their own lives, otherwise interest, motivation, and attention will be low. Start with a discussion of the benefits of the subject for them as individuals. Why not allocate, for example, the first period in any new school year to a discussion on why the students should devote their time and effort for the rest of the year to the subject? Let them use imagery to visualize the benefits and feelings of a successful outcome to their learning.

The actual environment should be relaxed and supportive, because we know that the brain actually "down-shifts" under stress to a more primitive survival mode. This restricts the use of the thinking cortex, and in extremes, the mind "goes blank". A relaxation exercise before learning is an effective tool.

There needs to be a specific provision for potentially distracting outside concerns to be brought up, voiced, and put aside. You cannot listen to two conversations at once. If the inner voice is competing for attention with worries or memories of past failure, the learner cannot hope to attend properly to incoming information.

2.   **Intake of Information**

A "big picture" overview of the subject should be presented first, because the "global" learners need this overall route map to see how it all fits together. They seek a pattern that makes sense.

Then new material needs to be presented to engage the visual, auditory and physical senses. One of the simplest aspects of learning style preference is the degree to which we need to initially see, hear, and get actively involved in what we are learning. Arthur Costa's work shows that a deliberate combination of all three methods of input ensures that this first preference is met.

Contrast this multi-sensory input to the one-dimensional approach of "Sit still, face the front, and listen to me."

3.   **Thinking about it**

One of the key characteristics of effective learners is the degree to which they elaborate on what they are learning, relating it to previous experience, existing knowledge, and constantly asking questions to ferret out the meaning. In other words they are not passive recipients of information, aiming at mere memorization, but active participants, turning it into personal understanding. Noel Entwistle characterizes this as "deep" versus "surface" learning.

It is at this elaboration, or "thinking about it," stage that Howard Gardner's concept of Multiple Intelligences is so useful, because it is actionable.

If the learner is given the opportunity to experience the subject through a planned cycle of activities that are designed to utilize all seven intelligences, we can be reasonably sure that the learning process will engage a wide range of learning styles.

To use Howard Gardner's own phrase, it is "Multiple Chance" education—as opposed to the "Single Chance" theory of education which is conventionally directed to primarily two intelligences—the linguistic and mathematical/logical.

"Single Chance" teaching, training, and learning rely over-heavily on lectures, texts, and a linear step-by-step revealing of the subject matter. We do not propose substituting for these vital intelligences and methods—but we do propose adding to them.

This means that a full cycle of elaborating activities should include opportunities, for example, to:

☐ Learn via pair and cooperative learning and games [inter-personal intelligence]

☐ Sit quietly, reflect and plan how to apply the learning [intra-personal intelligence]

☐ Engage in role play, experiential work and mental rehearsal [kinesthetic intelligence]

☐ Create mental images, mindscapes, graphs, posters, drawings and charts [visual/spatial intelligence]

☐ Memorize material in raps, songs or jingles, or conduct a mental review of the content of the study period over a background of classical music [musical intelligence].

At the most basic level of argument it seems clear that adding the power of five other forms of intelligence to the "conventional" two should logically produce superior results. There are then enough ways to "get it" so all main learning preferences are accommodated.

The secret is not to worry about each person's individual learning preference—which would be impractical—but to incorporate a planned cycle that covers them all. The more ways you teach, the more people you reach.

We have direct experience that learners really do feel empowered when they recognize that they have a range of talents to apply. Self limits start to disappear when they appreciate that previous poor learning experiences may have been due to the fact that the teaching style was too narrow to have accommodated their learning style.

Learners can be helped to assess their preferred learning styles and strengths, and then taught ways to adapt the learning situation so that they use their strengths and work to improve their weaker areas.

Coupled with the opportunity to use the full range of intelligences is the need to deliberately engage the emotions in a positive manner. Research by Paul McLean and others at the US National Institute of Mental Health, has shown that the mid-brain, or limbic system, is not only a controller of our emotions and immune system, but that an important aspect of long-term memory is located there, in the amygdala and hippocampus.

Emotions and long-term memory are directly linked. This neatly explains why we remember things with emotional significance—our first kiss, for example, or why a certain song can bring back vivid memories.

The implication for learning is that we cannot teach to the cerebral cortex alone. The part of the brain that processes emotions is inevitably involved. Indeed, recent research indicates that, when humans are exposed to material in a form that creates positive emotions—including music, art and drama—learning becomes not only more pleasurable but more efficient. Positive emotions play an important role in making learning faster and easier as well as improving memory and retention.

As we begin to understand the mind such results are more understandable. When a human mind listens to a piece of music or interprets the nuances of a play or work of art, it is learning to interpret complex data and take creative action. These are precisely the higher order thinking skills needed to learn a computer program or deal with a challenging work plan. Indeed, with the use of Positron Emission Tomography (a PET scan), we can actually see a brain working. The same areas of the brain are active when mathematical reasoning is going on as when a musician is reading and playing his part.

This is why we need to ensure that lesson content is delivered in ways that actively engage the emotions. It is, therefore, no mystery why people learn well through games, art activities and stories, or why a musical background to a review session improves retention.

"People learn in direct proportion to how much fun they are having," says corporate trainer Bob Pike. Now we know why. If history were only taught as a story of the ambitions, follies, and inspirational actions of the people involved it would be a popular subject indeed.

The third stage of learning, then, needs to ensure that new knowledge is acted on, manipulated, and elaborated by the seven intelligences, and that ways are found to involve positive emotions.

4.   **Store it**

If the first three stages of the model of learning have been thoroughly understood and implemented by **both** the learner and the teacher—the subject will have been presented in a brain-friendly manner and therefore well-learned. Associations and memories should have been created in several areas of the brain.

Nevertheless, the rate of forgetting can still be high, unless there is a specific attempt to consolidate the knowledge. The learner needs some sort of summary that "triggers" the whole of what has been learned. Learners benefit from mnemonics, mind maps, and what we call a review "concert," in which a summary is spoken over a background of specially selected classical music.

5.   **Practice it**

Towards the end of each learning session, there needs to be an opportunity for the learner to put his or her knowledge into practice. This can be in the form of a written, spoken, or physical demonstration to show that information has been acquired or behavior has changed.

The explicit intention of this stage is not to test for "right" or "wrong," but to provide the learner with a feedback on what is working and what is not.

In this way errors are seen, and even appreciated, as useful guidance on the need for a change in approach, not as a threat or a negative. The assumption is that time is the only variable in ultimate success, and that errors are a staging post on that journey.

6.   **Review**

After every learning situation there always needs to be a period of reflection—a chance for the learners to consider on what methods are working for them—and what needs improvement.

This stage is a critical one in the creation of self-directed learning.

There are at least two successful methods. The first involves the use of a Personal Progress Plan, a way to record conclusions, make plans for improvement, involve mentors, and work out how to overcome obstacles. It is at this point that the importance of a self reward for each step of progress can be introduced. The second method is to use a "study buddy," a partner with whom the learner can talk out his or her conclusions and understandings.

Robert Sternberg has shown how important articulation is in learning. When learners talk through what they have learned aloud, it not only ensures that they marshall their thoughts properly, it provides an additional auditory association for what they are learning.

A particularly powerful piece of evidence in favor of reviewing in a small group comes from a study by behavioral psychologist Kurt Lewin. He demonstrated that when a subject was learned and then discussed it was ten times more likely to be acted on than when the subject was presented without the opportunity for discussion and, therefore, group commitment.

This simple built-in cycle of **do/review** reinforces the point that action without reflection does not lead to much progress. And theorizing without action is not usually very practical. You need both.

This, then, is the Six-Step model of learning that we propose. Its value, we believe, is that it is quite comprehensive yet easy to understand and act on. It has formed the underpinning design for a series of self study programs—for foreign languages, mathematics, art and, especially, Learning-to-Learn.

It also has formed the basis for a Training and Development Program. This program provides a framework into which trainers can fit existing materials. It is designed to help them meet the range of learning preferences in their classes by presenting to all the senses, and through elaboration activities that involve all the intelligences. All in a low threat, high energy environment, conducive to effective learning.

Evidence suggests it works. When pilot courses at Bell Atlantic Telephone were converted to this "Accelerated Learning" format, training times and costs were halved and employee performance improved significantly.

The creation of a national and corporate culture of lifelong learning requires people that have both the will and the skill to learn. We hope that by helping to lay bare the actual process of learning, both trainers and learners will see how to improve their performance at each stage. In practical application of these methods we are finding that both motivation and competence rise significantly.

When we developed the Six-Stage model of learning some two years ago, we called it System 2000, because the new millenium is almost here.We do not need to wait until then to apply strategies that make it possible for all students to learn successfully.

Linda A. Tsantis

Dr. Linda Tsantis is vice-president of America Tomorrow, an electronic network connecting education, business, and community leaders with leading-edge information on human development, learning, and cultural change. Previously, she was Senior Education Planner with the Washington Center for Technology in Education, IBM Education Systems, where she guided a variety of IBM education initiatives involving federal agencies and education associations.

After graduating and receiving her master's degree from Old Dominion University, she received her doctorate in Special Education from George Washington University. She continued her post-doctoral studies at Harvard University, in Infant and Toddler Education; at Columbia University, in Neuroscience and Education; at Harvard Medical School, in Affective Development in Infancy and Early Childhood; and at George Washington University, in Computer Literacy.

Beginning her career as a Head Start teacher, she became an educational diagnostician at Georgetown University Hospital, then joined the faculty of George Washington University where she taught for fourteen years before moving to IBM in 1984 as an Academic Specialist.

Also in 1984 she received the "Excellence in Education" Citation for Outstanding Teacher Training Program from the Office of Special Education Programs of the US Department of Education. She was honored by the Council for Exceptional Children in 1987 for her work in developing Project RETOOL: Training in Special Education Technology for Faculty Teacher Trainers.

Dr. Tsantis' current projects explore the role of technology in neuroscience applications affecting transformational learning. Her work addresses the use of an intergenerational approach in breaking the cycle of disadvantage for low-income families.

TECHNOLOGY AS THE CATALYST   Linda A. Tsantis, Ph.D.

Education has historically prepared most students to live productive lives in a family within a society. Throughout most of history the definition of the terms "productive," "family," and "society" have been quite stable or at least predictable. In the agrarian society, most people found work in their local community and often worked in small groups made up of people who were also relatives. Many people rarely ventured more than a few miles from their home; their macro view of "the world" and their micro view of the family were highly convergent. Educational systems for this era involved broad, general curricula.

141

The industrial society saw many families leave their traditional homes and move to other locations where they could find work. Often they would take parents, brothers, and sisters along, and the moves ranged from just a few miles to between continents. Newspapers, radio and the telephone brought increased daily awareness of events in other locales, and the macro view became quite distinct and separate from the micro environment. The education system expanded the number and types of courses available to meet the needs of increasing numbers of special skills which this age required.

The information society has caused a dramatic shift in most of the paradigms on which our traditional views of society are based. We now share instant communications around the entire globe, ship products wherever there are buyers, and purchase goods and even "fresh foods" from other lands as often as from our own. Major new industries arrive or vanish overnight, families are spread across continents, and it is hard to establish the boundaries of a society. Virtually the only predictable trend is continuing change. The macro view of most individuals now encompasses the whole world, and the micro view is dangerously close to focusing only on the individual.

The implication for educators is clear—we must rethink most of our existing educational paradigms, for they are based on views of society that are no longer valid. Students must be prepared to accept, adapt to, and thrive upon change. The process of education must deal with the needs of students to develop both macro and micro strategies for dealing with their world.

Noted astronomer/educator Dr. Richard Berendzen expresses these needs eloquently: "We must learn to live as one family in our fragile, interdependent world, or we will surely perish;" and at a micro level: "The greatest classrooms of this nation or any nation are not in any school or any university. They're around the dinner tables in the homes. Insofar as global education is to be enriched and supported, education generally must too be nurtured. The issue is to deal not just with schools but also with homes and families." The industry in which I work as an educator both instigates and is in turn affected by the impact of information technology on society. Computer systems are at the heart of the paradigm shift from "manpower" to "mindpower" in the workplace around the globe.

One effect of the worldwide information processing capability is that work can now move to wherever skilled labor is available. Countries are now linked financially, economically, socially, culturally, and politically as never before, and this linkage is constantly growing. This can create new income and demand for more goods and services in countries which have educated their populations to deliver the skills in demand for the information age; it can rapidly drain countries whose citizens do not develop skills to keep pace with the emerging work opportunities.

Businesses today need a global perspective, and this globalization is changing the nature of competition and establishing more rigorous standards of quality in products, services, and solutions. Companies are learning that if they do not make use of the best available resources, their competition will, whether they are across town or across the world. Change has become a way of life, and he who masters change, wins.

The challenge to educators is clear. We must also establish rigorous standards of quality in the products, services, and solutions we offer to our youth. We must learn how to prepare all of our students for lives that are becoming more and more complex. We must prepare our students to master change.

Graduates must be prepared to deal with macro issues affecting their place in the world as well as micro issues affecting the quality of their lives. IBM Vice President Lucie Fjeldstad expresses the need as follows: "For IBM and companies like it around the globe, a world-class, competitive workforce and an informed consumer population is a strategic imperative—a matter of our very survival."

It is not going to be an easy task for education to accept and even welcome change, because of the sense of impermanence and discomfort which will naturally result. Furthermore, marked changes in attitudes, life styles, health care, financial stability, and marketplace behavior cannot be predicted by trends because these changes either create new trends or they alter trends already in place. Science historian Thomas Kuhn writes that when a critical mass of involved problems creates enough uneasiness within a community, certain kinds of people are going to search for a new paradigm to replace their existing and now dysfunctional set of assumptions; Kuhn has dubbed these people "paradigm pioneers". These change agents serve an essential role in shifting outmoded educational paradigms to ones that are truly appropriate for our times.

How Technology Supports A Paradigm Shift

It is increasingly difficult for traditional teaching techniques to capture and hold the interest of a child who has been reared on video games and MTV. Many educators believe multimedia technology can provide the teaching tool base needed to reach these students. This technology combines computers and voice, animated images, music, words and databases with teacher-friendly authoring systems. Increasingly such technology is being used in connection with powerful expert systems, which provide teachers (or students) with the opportunity to design approaches or check their thinking with the help of a body of rules developed by educators who are content experts.

144

This technology can serve as a catalyst to help educators capitalize on the unique skills which each learner brings to the classroom. Multimedia technology can support an education environment in which:

- ☐ All children can learn—the computer can enhance the learning process, from enabling communication for a child who is severely disabled, to providing insight and new ways of dynamically visualizing concepts for children who have special talents.

- ☐ Cultural heritages are valued and nurtured—technology can help teachers provide learning environments that are not only culturally sensitive to the heritage of each of their students, but culturally affirmative and rich in varied language experiences.

- ☐ Learning is a lifelong process—the computer can engage both parent and child and encourage learning for both through intergenerational sharing of language and experience.

- ☐ Families can become more self-sufficient—computer technology can provide individualized programs in basic skills, literacy, health and nutrition, and career development, not only in formal education environments, but in community centers, museums, libraries, and the home.

Our goal must be to harness technology to provide the most engaging and dynamic system ever used in education, so that school once again embraces culture and learning in our society.

James Botkin

In the report *No Limits to Learning*, which Dr. James Botkin co-authored for the Club of Rome, a primary feature of innovative learning is described as anticipation—preparing people to use techniques such as forecasting, simulations, scenarios, and models. Anticipatory learning encourages them to consider trends, to make plans, to evaluate future consequences and possible injurious side-effects of present decisions, and to recognize the global implications of local, national, and regional actions.

The book describes another primary feature of innovative learning as participation. "More than the formal sharing of decision, it is an attitude characterized by cooperation, dialogue, and empathy. It means not only keeping communications open but also constantly testing one's operating rules and values, retaining those that are relevant and rejecting those that have become obsolete."

Neither anticipation nor participation are new concepts by themselves, but what Dr. Botkin points out as new and vital for innovative learning is the insistence that they be tied together. The focus of his career has been on innovative learning in whatever capacity he has worked.

Dr. Botkin is co-founder of the Technology Resources Group, a partnership he established to conduct executive education, research, writing, and consulting. He is also the co-founder and president of the International Corporate Learning Association and Program Director for the Consortium Senior Managers Development Programme sponsored by the International Management Institute in Geneva. He was the first Executive Director and Director of Research for the Alliance for Learning, a consortium of AT&T, DuPont, General Motors, and Sears.

In addition to *No Limits to Learning*, Dr. Botkin co-authored *Global Stakes: The Future of High Technology in America*; *The Innovators: Rediscovering America's Creative Energy*; and *The New Alliance: Industry-University Partnerships*.

NO LIMITS TO LEARNING

James W. Botkin, Ph.D.

Ten years have passed since the first appearance of the Club of Rome's report, *No Limits to Learning* (English language edition, Pergamon Press, 1979; twelve other languages, 1980). Have we made any progress in rolling back limits imposed by outmoded organization and self-imposed outdated models of thinking? Have the concepts highlighted by the report, of anticipatory and participatory learning stood the test of a decade? Answers to both questions are "Yes," but the pace and manner have been slower and more varied than expected (by this author, at least). And leadership has come from an unexpected source—namely, the international business community.

First, readers may be interested to know what has become of the Club of Rome, which initiated the report, since it has not made headline news in recent years. In 1984, the founder and president of the Club, Aurelio Peccei, passed away. Stewardship of the Club passed to Alex King, a British scientist and cofounder of the Club, and headquarters moved to Paris. In 1988, the Club marked its 20th anniversary with a meeting in Paris hosted by the President of France. Participants took the occasion to visit UNESCO, where Club member Federico Mayor is Director General.

The Club has been quietly renewing its 100 members, seeking more representation from developing countries, more women, and more younger people. There has been considerable activity in Africa and the Soviet Union. In 1989, at a meeting hosted by Mikhail Gorbachev, the members of the Executive Council voted unanimously to select a new president, Ricardo Diez Hochleitner from Spain. He is a former State Minister of Education of Spain, head of the Spanish Chapter of the Club of Rome, and tireless worldwide activist.

One might reconsider for a moment the statement above that the Club of Rome has not been headline news. This is true in that the organization has been in a period of stewardship, but it has not been true outside the American press. Russian, Chinese, French, and African agencies have reported on the global activities of the Club of Rome, while the U.S. press continues to have its blinders well affixed.

Similar statements could be made about the field of learning and education. While other countries undertake reforms in their education, the United States continues to speak strongly and let its massive educational bureaucracy slide into increasing ineffectiveness. Few other nations have as large a schooling system as the American one, and among industrial countries, few are as deeply mired in decline as the US K-12 public/private school system.

Most American universities, still admired as among the top in the world, are not yet aware of the rapid changes among European and Asian universities, which are becoming more internationalized. If the rankings of top universities which are conducted annually in the US were done on a worldwide basis, America would still have a strong showing, but would probably not occupy the top positions. An example may illustrate this statement. Recently I was asked to organize a consortium of four management schools for a global executive education program. We started with the International Management Institute in Geneva, Switzerland. We linked to Sophia University in downtown Tokyo and to the newly-formed International Management Center in Budapest, Hungary. No suitable American partner willing to cooperate could be located. "They're all too parochial," noted a prominent international educator.

Here are some lessons that stand out for me since collaborating on *No Limits to Learning*:

Most Formal Schooling Systems, With Some Notable Exceptions, Resist Change In Their Objectives and Style of Learning and Education.

School, on a worldwide basis, is hopelessly out of date. In North America, despite widespread recognition of the inadequacy of K-12 and higher education, the response to date has been limited to "more" for the future of what has not worked in the recent past. More hours, more homework, more science and math have been the guiding principles rather than new teamwork, focus on values, or holistic learning. No country in the world has been able to figure out how to divest itself of a system built for another age and another time and to start afresh in redesigning formal education. In my exper-ience, the only countries that have even attempted something signi-ficant—and also with limited results—have been Japan, Austria, and Finland.

149

Schools and Universities Still Do Not Have the Financial or Innovative Human Resources to Carry Out, or Even Consider, the Fundamental Changes Needed to Meet the Challenge of the 21st Century.

Ministries of Education still play second or third fiddle to those of Defense or Finance. Meanwhile, problems of drugs, dropouts, and deprivation go universally unchallenged as a growing fact of classroom life in all western countries. Even our most prestigious and wealthy world-class universities seem paralyzed and unable to provide leadership for a new era of innovative learning.

The Place Where There Is Promising Action in Reforming Education and Modernizing Learning Is the International Business Community.

It comes as a surprise to traditional educators to learn that fully one-third of professional educators are at work not in universities but in corporate institutes of education. Another one-third are in church-related education, and the balance in conventional public and private educational institutions.

Business, which has become the front line for human resources and personnel development, has taken up the challenges raised in *No Limits to Learning* in ways unforeseen by many. This is increasingly accomplished through alliances and consortia, and the agenda is "new learning for the 90's." An example of this approach is InterCLASS—the International Corporate Learning Association— which I have recently launched with Eric Vogt in Cambridge, Massachusetts, and Santa Fe, New Mexico. The purpose of InterCLASS is to provide advanced learning services to its corporate members and to develop the discipline of corporate, or group, learning.

150

Predecessor groups to InterCLASS are the Alliance for Learning in North America, the Scandinavian Leadership Initiative in Northern Europe, and the ongoing CSMDP program that operates in Geneva, Boston, Tokyo, and Budapest. These and other groups explore, through teaching and research, new and "cutting edge" techniques of personal effectiveness in the areas of globalization, the future, and teamwork. Their goal: to make innovative learning an integral force for world development, now and into the next century.

In sum, the eighties brought widespread awareness of the need for changes in our patterns of learning. Who in the nineties will begin to act on that awareness?

Anne Taylor

"Before Western civilization divided the Universe into discrete subject matter areas, the order in the Universe was (and still is) both interdisciplinary and holistic. The branching of trees, spiraling of shells, meandering of streams, and the radial designs of flowers, for example, represent an a synthesis of mathematics, biology and art. The current artificial separation of subject matter is in contrast to the way the world is constructed and the way children perceive it. Architecture and the built environment synthesize the world of ideas and the world of material things. They help us to realize that we are a part of, not apart from, the environment." So speaks Anne Taylor.

She is a professor in the School of Architecture and Planning and co-director of the Institute for Environmental Education at the University of New Mexico. She is also visiting professor at the College of Architecture and Urban Planning at the University of Washington. For twenty years she and architect George Vlastos have worked to research and design learning environments and their effects. They are co-authors of *School Zone: Learning Environments for Children*, and are also co-authors of a curriculum series to teach architecture and design to teachers and children. They have designed a Head Start Classroom for the Future, and created a special modular system of early childhood portable furniture.

Dr. Taylor is founder and program director of the Architecture and Children Institute based both in New Mexico and in the state of Washington. In both states she trains teachers in the Architecture for Children curriculum, which is an interdisciplinary curriculum model used as a basis for design so that math, science, social studies, and art are taught through architecture.

After graduating from the Eastman School of Music and Wells College, she received her master's and doctorate in Art Education/Architecture from Arizona State University.

152

THE ECOLOGY OF THE LEARNING ENVIRONMENT

Anne Taylor, Ph.D.

The Current State of Learning Environments

In 1980, 75% of the schools in New York had been built before 1900. In 1990, 61% of our nation's schools were constructed in the 1950's and 60's. The construction was rapid and cheap, built to last 30 years. Their time is up—20% are older than fifty years, and only 6% were built in the eighties. Of the total number of inadequate school buildings, 61% need major repairs, 43% are obsolete, 42% have environmental hazards, 25% are overcrowded, and 13% are structurally unsound.

With increasing enrollments, California will need 800 new schools by 1993, and Florida will need 816 new schools within ten years. New programs in schools will require additional space to house them. These include special education, science/math labs, technology/computer labs, and the performing arts. Yet the Education Writers Association "could not locate a comprehensive university program specifically for school facility planning" during their research done earlier this year.

In the past, educators and architects had a predetermined vision of what schools should be. Educational specifications were written for the architect as if there were a form for school design which included so many look-alike classrooms, hallways, gymnasiums, cafeterias for institutional food distribution, and administrative offices. The playground was a forgotten piece of property, even though it was often the most valuable piece of land in the neighborhood. Instead of being used as a landscape design for learning, it was a barren patch of ground encompassed by a chain link fence.

America, as well as the rest of the world, is on the brink of an educational facility facelift. There is a revolution in learning under way. It promises to move both the state of the art for redesigned schools and also children into the 21st century at a rapid rate. The new discoveries underlying the revolution document beyond question that human infants and children learn more rapidly in stimulating and varied physical environments which meet basic human needs. The results of this research are being applied to a very old challenge—the renovation, rethinking, and redesign of schools for children and their parents.

The historic design assumes that educational architecture is a series of empty boxes into which "school furniture" is placed. Even new schools place students in straight rows, facing front, learning mainly from textbooks which, because of state laws, still dominate the classroom. The computer is an adjunct to learning and often "down the hall" in a room where children go in groups of thirty to learn technical skills. The American school, an environment in which children spend a large share of their time for over eighteen years and beyond, leaves little room for self-expression and a sense of ownership or involvement. Yet actually there cannot be separation between the learning process and the physical environment—they are integral parts of each other.

Many architects who have been commissioned by school districts to design "a school of the future" are puzzled because of the old educational specifications with prescribed and predetermined square footage needs, which are now no longer viable. Architects want educators to envision with them what the school of the future will be. But the educators are having a difficult time articulating the educational program of the future, its curriculum and instructional methodology. Unfortunately, because no one can foresee the future, bond issues are being passed and construction is under way using outdated models and design formats which are over 200 years old.

Though these schools may have a slick post-modern entryway and a bit more landscaping, the innovation is not creative enough. One superintendent in Washington State fired three architects, saying that their solutions for future classroom and school design were not innovative or creativive. That same district, however, replicated one school five times without performing a post-occupancy evaluation on the first prototype to see whether it needed work.

Learning Environments Can Teach

In our work, architect George Vlastos and I have spent over twenty years researching and designing indoor and outdoor learning environments as functional art forms, places of beauty, and motivational centers for learning. We have used the architecture of the school classroom, museum exhibits, and the landscape as a means of demonstrating how the built and natural environments demonstrate, in real live form, the ideas, laws and principles that we at present are trying to teach children from textbooks.

For instance, a solar greenhouse can help children nourish life outside themselves, understand botany, and begin to learn about alternative energy systems. Its systems can be studied and compared to body systems. Children can graph and understand plant growth, classify and compare it, and harvest food. A cooking environment can provide science and math learning, cultural uses of food, and the creativity of edible art.

The structure of the building itself can teach physics, concepts of tension, compression, force, load cantilevering, fenestration patterns, the awareness of solids/voids and massing as a basis for descriptive geometry. The electrical mechanical system, if left open for children to see, can be a lesson in the input and output systems that are similar to the arteries and veins in our bodies. The acreage surrounding a school, oftentimes a valuable but neglected piece of flat property, can be redesigned with the help of a landscape architect. It can become a "landscape for learning" and an open park for the community. Hills, valleys, deciduous trees, non-deciduous trees, gardens, and graphics, all become learning tools.

Creating Learning Environments

In designing buildings, it is essential to study the *client*, his special needs, spaces needed to support activities, and aesthetic preferences. In the case of a school, the *clients* are the children. Teachers are clients too, but the favored client is the child. Therefore, in writing a program for the architectural design, one needs to study

the *curriculum content* and the *developmental needs* of the children as
the design determinants. These developmental needs fall into a
body, mind, spirit continuum. Information is extrapolated from
these two sources, as well as information and ideas from children as
to their preferences, likes, dislikes, and their innovative ideas for
learning environments.

In a small rural school in Trout Lake, Washington, the total
faculty and 150 children were trained to use architecture and design
as a way to teach basic skills. The community had defeated a bond
issue for a new school building over a period of six years. The
teachers and children spent the year collecting data, writing about
and drawing architectural concepts in plan view and elevation.
Using this they built models to depict their ideas for a new school.
A community meeting was held to involve the citizens of that area
in a discussion of their preferences as well. An art and architectural
exhibition of the children's work, including computer graphics
executed by high school students, was displayed.

One month later the bond issue was passed and all parties look
forward, not to a traditional school, but to an intergenerational
community center. High school students are working with the Forest
Service to do an environmental impact study on the chosen site.
The architect is planning to come to the school and show students
how to use computer-assisted design as he does the working drawings.

Some direct spin-offs from Trout Lake include these steps:
Architecture and Design will be incorporated into the fifth and sixth
grade curriculum; IBM discs from the architect with project
information will enable everyone to keep pace with developments
using the computer programs; students will be engaged in
landscaping and construction of play areas, observatories, and nature
walks at the new school site; mechanical drawing class will switch
to CAD drafting during the 2nd semester; students will be using a

computer program called "SIMCITY" as part of their civics class to design a model city responding to its dilemmas.

Classrooms for the Future

The twenty-first century stands right before us. The decisions we make today and the actions we take tomorrow will set the tone for the direction of our schools in the coming decades.

Primary needs include the remodeling of current classrooms, the designing and building of new schools, and a rethinking of what "school" means in light of the changes we foresee in the near future. Perhaps schools won't look like schools. Perhaps we will be using the total community as a learning environment—not a new idea.

Although we would like to see schools not stereotyped by lockstep classroom configuration, we know that classrooms are probably here to stay. It is possible, however, to rethink their design and the components which make up the classroom of the future.

Borrowing from many areas of study, one envisions classrooms and playground as living museums, studios, and laboratories for hands-on learning with a computer for every student, tele-communications studios for world-wide communication, and interactive video for encyclopedia verbal-visual information retrieval. Learning materials include computer discs, video cassettes, good children's literature, music, photographs, paintings, found objects, toys, games, creative materials, and natural materials systematically and hierarchically assembled, based on themes or concepts of known interest to children, perhaps retrievable by computer.

Should it not be possible for present and future learning environments to include communication centers with the use of printing presses, computers, televisions, and radio; art, music, and dance studios open and available at all times; creative dramatics as an everyday pursuit; and cooking-science areas? Portable mini-environments that are thematically designed and fully equipped could travel from school to school, expanding our children's experience of being involved and capable in many different types of environments. They might even be responsible for designing and maintaining the architectural setting.

In our workshops and seminars where teachers and children were asked to re-design their classrooms for the future, many unique design ideas have emerged beyond the given developmental and curricular determinants.

Some of the following represent those ideas:

1. Eliminate desks and substitute other personal space storage and writing surfaces.

2. Design light and moveable partitions. Children will be moving through the environment in the future.

3. Create mobile furniture that has multiple uses for children.

4. Create an environment that is receptive to new technology and electronic devices.

5. Create stackable seating scaled to children.

6. Provide for privacy in the classroom. Corners are relatively unused spaces which could be privacy "relief" places. Some children learn better by themselves or in small groups in private spaces.

7. Use innovative storage systems for tables and computers to free space for other activities.

8. Give heating, cooling, plumbing information in the architecture by leaving a portion exposed.

9. Design colorful, attractive, and hospitable hallways.

10. Design a velcro wall to which special instructional items can be attached.

11. Design hallway graphics and mini-museums.

The rationale for this programming process is based on research from the field of Design and Behavior, which shows that if a learning environment is designed based on what is taught and learned, and if the facilities or adjacent spaces reflect concepts and principles to be learned, then both behavior and learning are affected by the design of the environment. This is a "whole system" view of learning that can make a critical difference in creating schools to meet the needs of today's and tomorrow's students.

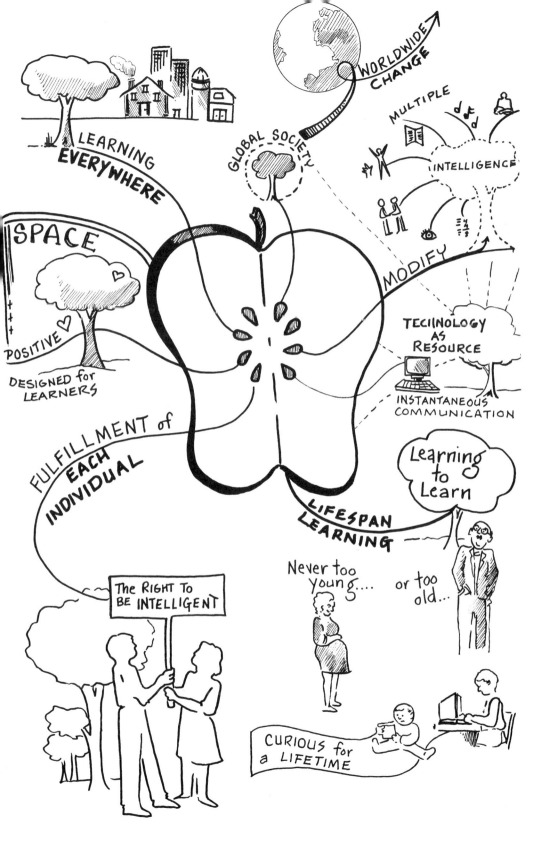

Shirley D. McCune

Dr. Shirley McCune's eyes sparkle when she speaks to teachers about their new role in new kinds of educational systems. She travels throughout the United States devoting herself to moving educational organizations forward, as she did in consulting with the Washington Education Association during the drafting of their innovative 1989 report, *Restructuring Public Education: Building a Learning Community.*

Dr. McCune is senior director with the Mid-continent Regional Educational Laboratory and director of the McREL Center for Educational Equity in Colorado. She is also the president of Learning Trends, a Denver-based research and development firm working to monitor societal and educational trends and identify their implications for educational policies, practices, and programs.

She graduated from the University of Northern Colorado, received her master's degree from the University of Denver, and her doctorate from Catholic University of America. She has been a classroom teacher, university faculty member, educational researcher, educational association manager, and federal executive.

In her recent monograph, published by the Association for Supervision and Curriculum Development and entitled *Guide to Strategic Planning for Educators,* she describes the focus of strategic planning as "a process powered by the basic human drive to solve problems—to eliminate discrepancies between what is and what must be. A primary value of strategic planning is that it forces people and institutions to reexamine, to refocus, and to seek out or create new means for accomplishing their purposes."

As a catalyst in that process, Dr. McCune has authored or co-authored numerous research reports, articles, and monographs. She is a change agent whose work in training, consulting, and planning conferences has resulted in action on the part of educators, state leaders and legislators, business organizations, and federal agencies.

162

Shirley McCune, Ph.D.

Education journals, reports, and dialogues among educators are filled with references to the need for and methods of restructuring education. Many different approaches are being implemented in state policies and local schools across the nation. The move toward educational restructuring often seems to be fragmented and unclear in its purpose and direction. It is as if we recognize the need for a new game but still have not quite figured out who the players are, where the game should be played, or by what rules. The following is an effort to identify the forces that require a new game and to outline some perspectives on the rules for the game and the selection of players. The need for the restructuring of education moves beyond the issues of educational reform. Any such restructuring must be grounded in a broad understanding of the basic contract between education and society and the ways that that contract and set of relationships must be changed to meet individual, community, and national needs.

The Need For Restructuring

The basic function of schools in any society is to socialize and prepare children and youth with the knowledge, attitudes, skills, and behaviors that they will need to fulfill their individual and societal roles as adults. Schools must do this by carrying out two paradoxical functions. On the one hand, schools must transmit and conserve the knowledge developed in the past. In this sense, schools are conserving institutions. On the other hand, schools must anticipate the future and the knowledge, skills, and behaviors that youth will need when they assume adult roles and then "backward map" in finding ways to prepare them for a future society. The transmission of past culture is a much easier task than anticipating how to prepare students for a future culture. As a result, many of our educational efforts are unbalanced in that students learn about the past but are not prepared to understand or deal with the needs of a future society.

The contract between schools and society is based on a set of goals fitting society's needs at a specific point in time. The basic structures of today's schools were formulated in the 1880s, when the goals were organized around the needs for developing a national set of values for the Americanization of immigrant groups, for preparing youth with basic skills to participate in work and in democratic activities, and for preparing some children for leadership positions. These basic purposes continue to shape American education more than 100 years later.

Our society has undergone profound economic, demographic, and social transformation—a transformation that impacts virtually every aspect of our individual and collective lives. It is the manifestation of a new era of civilization—one produced by the cumulative build up of technological change. The information age has rapidly moved powerfully into place in the restructuring of the economy and the movement from a national to a global society. Virtually every institution is forced to restructure to meet a changed environment and changed needs. The total society is struggling with a crisis in restructuring.

Education is not immune from the need for restructuring and the pressures for it. In fact, the new society, the information society, places education and training in a position of greater importance. Two primary resources are required for any group or society to succeed in an information age. These are information capital, or the ability to apply and extend information in the development of new or better products and services, and human capital, or the ability to produce citizens who are highly skilled and have the ability to process and apply information. Schools, training programs, and institutions have the basic responsibility for human capital development and, to some extent, the responsibility for information capital or knowledge creation. Thus, critical needs of the society must be met by education and training institutions.

Some people believe societal needs can be met by fixing up or improving present educational structures, programs, and practices. Educational improvement approaches serve a need, but they are insufficient to meet the need for transformed educational systems which match the transformations of the larger society. Only when the basic mismatch between the current industrial-based education system and the new requirements for an educational system designed for an information society are met, will schools be able to prepare children and adults for living productive and fulfilling lives.

Forces For Restructuring

A first step in any educational restructuring is to gain an understanding of societal transformations and the implications raised for the restructuring of schools. Five societal transformations create pressures for change and begin to shape the necessary directions for educational restructuring. These five forces—economic, social demographic, organizational, educational, and individual—help us to establish the context and general directions for restructuring education.

Economic Forces

The most basic change in the economic sector has been the fundamental change in the nature of work. Physical work of the industrial age has been replaced by mind and service work. Employers need people who can solve problems, develop new products and ways of working and providing services, and organize and process information in new ways.

Robert R. Carkhuff has described the shift in industry by pointing out that the basis for productivity has changed. In the 1950s productivity was achieved by working harder—adding to the number of hours of work, involving more people in the task. This approach has some value but it is expensive and often does not result in real productivity increases. By the 1980s we had discovered that productivity gains could best be produced by working smarter. We were forced to find methods of production which used information to increase productivity. In the 1990s, productivity gains will be based on thinking better and being able to process complex information about multiple systems. It will require persons with generalized and specialized knowledge and the ability to think and process across an organization or across multiple levels of systems.

Carkhuff goes on to articulate the need for individual change. He outlines three phases and approaches to education and training. These are outlined as follows:

Development Of Educational Goals And Approaches

Industrial Age

Stimulus ——————— Response

Goal: Reduce the number of responses

Early Information Age

Stimulus ——————— Responses

Goal: To increase alternatives for response

Later Information Age

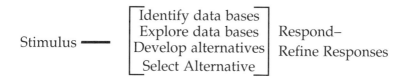

Goal: To complete full information processing

We can see that the work productivity goals of working harder, working smarter, and thinking better are paralleled by the individual goals of limiting responses to increasing alternatives and complete information processing. It is also evident that the goals of education and training activities change dramatically. The industrial age goal of reducing responses was a part of the needs for standardization and synchronization. It was based on the assumption of a stable environment where the task was to ensure the "right" response. In education this was seen in a "one-way" approach—there was one right answer, and classroom activities (including testing) were designed to reinforce the rightness of that approach.

Today, we live in an ever-changing environment. The task of the school must be to help students learn to recognize differences and be able to analyze the situation and make a large number of decisions or discriminations. The basic goal and purpose of education has changed dramatically, as has the complexity of the learning task.

Economic forces require that schools prepare students with more than the memorization of facts. Students must have the ability to understand numerous variables and be able to process data in effective ways. They must be able to work at recognizing relationships and connections among seemingly disparate items and events. This requires a level of cognitive skills that were considerably beyond the goals articulated for education and training efforts.

Social/Demographic Forces

America's population, like other sectors of our society, is being transformed. When we examine the demographic changes in our society, we find that the population is growing older; it is increasingly ethnically/racially diverse, and the numbers of poor children and families continue to increase. Two primary social structures—the family and the community—are fragmented, and the systems for the socialization of youth and community support have deteriorated.

Much of the impact of this deterioration is manifested in schools. Nearly 25% of our children are poor, an estimated 30% of them are sexually, physically, or emotionally abused, the time that parents spend with children has declined, and the numbers of children with permanent drug, alcohol, and other forms of mental and behavioral disorders seem to be increasing.

The schools have taken on some of the emotional and physical problems of children. School nutrition programs, provision of special education programs, increased counselling and psychological services have been established. Much of this is inadequate to meet the needs of the at risk or the average child. What has become apparent is that we can no longer fragment human services for children. Learning is a process which requires basic levels of physical functioning. Teaching must be provided within the frame of reference of the student, and teachers must recognize that the doorway or precondition for learning is the affective climate of the classroom.

Changes in the goals of education and the conditions of children's lives require that schools view children and the teaching/ learning process in new ways. Schools must not be bound by bureaucratic and professional boundaries and norms. They must be fully responsive to the range of needs that children are experiencing. The school is moving out of the business of "schooling" into the business of human resource development. Some will question the need for an expanded role for schools. The answers must be found in the need for a holistic approach to growth and learning and the reality that the public schools continue to be the only comprehensive delivery system of services to children.

A related task that must become a part of the public schools is that of early childhood education for three to five year olds. Much

169

of a child's potential for learning and development is determined by the developmental experiences he or she has had between three and five years of age. Developmentally oriented programs that highlight the physical, social, and language growth of young children is essential if American children are to meet the expanded goals of education. A network of public and private early childhood services is essential if we are to meet the early preconditions for learning.

Organizational Forces

Perhaps the most unrecognized transformation within our society has been the restructuring of organizations and ways of work. Most of us perceive the widespread decentralization of organizations, the need for organizational flexibility, and the requirements for participative management. What is not recognized is the impact of these changes on the roles of educators, the need for new organizational values and for new sets of relationships and organizational behaviors.

Many school systems recognize the need for organizational change and renewal, and we see an expansion of strategic planning and site-based management. Appropriate as these efforts are, there is little recognition of the amount of effort required to achieve widespread organizational change. Few site-based management efforts or implementation plans have been successful. There is often an assumption that when people know what to do, they will be able to do it. While there are a comparatively few educators with the knowledge and skills required for working in a network type, organization rather than a bureaucracy, many are unable to function in this new organizational form.

If an organization is to renew itself, it must become serious about supporting and empowering employee and governance development. The organization itself must become a learning and knowledge creation organization. In essence, the organization must play a critical role in individual empowerment and change.

The scope of this task is frequently underestimated. A model of change requirements developed by McCune suggests that the following steps are needed for organization change.

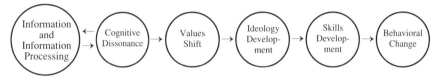

The model outlines the ongoing need for information and the processing of information. They may produce or be the result of cognitive dissonance. Efforts must be given to a basic shift in the organizations' and individuals' values. The shift in values is made real only when an ideology specifies the rationale for the shift and the implications for daily operations. The skills development of staff and governance is an essential task if the organization is to change. Ultimately, these steps lead to changed behaviors and a changed organization.

Some of the critical shifts that must take place, as summarized by Hallett, are outlined in the following chart:

Shifts in Organizational Norms and Values

Organizational Elements	Industrial Age	Information Age
Organizational Structure	Bureaucracy	Connected networks
Individual's World View	Organization as a source of security and self esteem	Organization as a tool for personal contributions
Size	Bigger is better	Small is beautiful
Responsibilities	Specialized	Generalized
Individual worth	Organizational status	Ability to use information and be productive
Focus	Organization	Customer
Style	Competitive internally and externally	Goal oriented, caring and collaborative

172

The organizational changes that are essential must be focused in the direction of creating a continually developing learning organization and of continuing the empowerment of staff and governance personnel.

Educational Forces

The restructuring of educational organizations is essential, but this is likely to have little effect unless we understand the need for the restructuring of our teaching assumptions and methods. The most basic form of restructuring is the redefinition of learning within educational practice.

Clarkhuff identifies three basic steps that are essential for learning. These are illustrated below.

Phases of Learning

Exploring ⟶ Understanding ⟶ Acting

Where they are   Where they want/   To get where they
               need to be   need/want to

This formulation of the learning process outlines the fact that learning is individualized and must be linked to the frame of reference and associations of the learner. A second feature of this formulation is that all learning culminates in some type of action. This is consistent with the definition of learning as a change in behavior.

Current American education focuses on the understanding phase of the learning process, with comparatively little attention being devoted to the individualization of learning or the application of information. This rote approach to learning results in an emphasis on the mastery of facts with little attention being given to the application of knowledge or the needs of the learner.

Although the goals of education (to prepare children and youth for adult life in an information society) remain the same, the basic values and outcomes must change to fit the needs of a new age. Examples of basic shifts which must be made are provided below.

Educational Values Shifts

From	To
Schooling	Learning
Accreditation	Performance
Schooling as preparation for adult roles	Continuing education
Limited achievement	No limits to learning
Sorting	Opportunity system
Picking "winners"	Developing "winners"
Measures of factual recall	Ability to process and apply information

These shifts require a thorough restructuring of not only schools but also the learning process. Teaching children how to learn, to process information, and to apply information calls for a more individualized, problem focused, integrated method of instruction. Carnegie units, and tests which basically only measure factual recall, must be replaced by new systems and structures. There are undoubtedly many ways that the classroom experience can be restructured; in any case, some of the key characteristics of restructuring must include:

New Facilities and Equipment

Classrooms should be informal, allowing for multi-purpose use. There should be seminar tables, carrels, work areas, and places to spread out for small group work.

Curriculum

The curriculum may be organized in any number of ways—around themes (magnets), special interests, alternative programs, or work in the community. It must develop interdisciplinary relationships and culminate in action or application activities if it is to be relevant to future needs.

Instruction

The expansion of instructional methodologies is an essential element of restructuring. Instruction must also begin with the frame of reference of the learner, be more explicit in outlining all of the steps necessary for learning, provide for different types of intelligence and learning styles, and focus on the processing of information rather than the memorization of facts.

School Management

School management must provide enough structure to ensure that children are learning and that the broad goals of the district are being met. It must also encourage greater freedom and autonomy for buildings and programs and enable staff and community to develop options at the building level.

These forms of restructuring are essential goals of preparing children and youth for a future society.

Individual Forces

A basic element of the restructuring of schools is that we must produce individuals who function at higher physical, emotional, and intellectual levels than most people do today. Life in a fast-moving technological society requires people who are skilled, flexible, able to tolerate stress and change, able to work collaboratively with others, yet able to maintain a strong sense of self. For persons with these characteristics, the next years are likely to be productive and fulfilling. For persons without these skills, life may be stressful and frustrating.

Our views of the types of competencies or outcomes which schools should produce have, up to now, been quite limited. We have generally focused on the attainment of a body of knowledge. Seldom have these bodies of information been provided to students in ways that would assist them in applying them in real life. Competencies and skills related to their personal life (self concept development, ethical development, life planning), their career development (learning to learn, career management, continuing education, experiential learning), and their knowledge of leadership, systems and groups (organizational structure and growth, working across cultures, interpersonal skills, participative management and leadership), must be an integral part of the teaching-learning process.

Not only must we help children develop their capacities more fully, but also we must find ways of increasing the knowledge, skills, and capabilities of today's adults. While this effort must be based on multiple strategies of individual staff development and special programs, greater attention must be given to organizational development. Organizations influence significant portions of our lives either positively or negatively. Major attention must be given to ways that the structures and operation of organizations may be used for further individual growth and development. If we can achieve this at high levels we will have created a new power, that of organizational capital.

Organizational capital will be achieved not by designating a few schools as site-based management schools, but by an in-depth restructuring of organizations and empowering of staff to provide a better and more satisfying quality of organizational life.

Responses to Restructuring

Many have been aware of the need for the restructuring of schools but have not been clear about how to approach the problem. Three major approaches have been used in restructuring. These are bringing the community to the school; restructuring the bureaucracy; and redesigning students' educational experience. Each is described below.

Bringing the Community to the School

Much of the initial educational restructuring grew out of strategic planning models that had been applied to education. Educators were aware that the support for schools has declined, largely as a function of the decline in households with school age children. In the 1950s, one out of two households had a school age child; today, it is one out of five. This decline has been a factor in the decreased support of schools.

Many looked at the community and began to realize the needs for services that schools could fulfill. New programs for new client groups were established to meet community needs. Some of the most obvious services schools could provide were early childhood education and latchkey programs. Services for senior citizens, adult job training, adult education, and a variety of other activities have opened the school to the community. The extension of this model is a learning community where persons of all ages are interacting in learning programs. The school is not simply a multi-function building but is a center where a wide variety of interactive, inter-generational programs are provided that can extend the learning of all groups.

Variations of this restructuring approach are found in business-partnerships, school without walls, business-based programs, and a number of other approaches.

The basic goals of this form of restructuring are related to the need for:

☐ Maintaining a sense of relevance to the needs of the community;

☐ Putting the school into the mainstream of the community;

☐ Increasing learning resources (human and fiscal); and

☐ Expanding the general support base for the schools.

Restructuring the Bureaucracy

A second and perhaps the most commonly understood meaning of restructuring is opening up the bureaucracy and decentralizing by allocating more power and autonomy at the building level. The movement known as site-based management is based on the recognition that a standardized, cookie-cutter approach to schools is not likely to meet student, staff, or neighborhood needs.

Site-based management is one of the needs that must be addressed in restructuring of schools. Too frequently, however, it is approached as a panacea without an overall understanding of the related changes which must be made if it is to be successful.

Site-based management requires a new set of organizational structures and relationships. The role of nearly everyone in the system is changed, and attention must be given to helping people learn new role behaviors. Site-based management inevitably requires a redistribution of power, and people must learn participative and inclusive management skills if it is to be successful.

Some have been encouraged by the initial successes of site-based management demonstrations. In these instances, the success can usually be traced to the knowledge and skills of a gifted principal. There will undoubtedly be a productivity increase when persons with unusual skills (less than 20% of administrators) move into a new freedom. If site-based management is to be an integral and ongoing characteristic of all schools, much work will be needed in individual and organizational development.

Restructuring the Teaching/Learning Process

Many have realized that while bringing the community into the school and redesigning the bureaucracy have many positive values, neither of these processes addresses the restructuring of the teaching-learning process in a direct way. Both approaches could be carried out successfully with benefits to the community and school staff, but little would be changed at the classroom level.

The restructuring at the classroom level must be based on the understanding that high levels of learning require a systematic and intense affective and cognitive interaction between teacher and students. It is the quality and intensity of this relationship that facilitates student learning. If this is to be provided to students, teachers likewise must have higher levels of emotional, physical, and fiscal support. In a sense, it is the task of everyone in the school and community system to support the teaching-learning process in the classroom in productive ways.

Examples of the key principles to be incorporated into the restructuring of the teaching/learning process include the following:

☐ All learning begins with the affective; strong interpersonal skills provided to children in an equitable way are necessary preconditions for affective learning;

☐ Language development is the essential element for academic and life achievement; all effective teaching must focus on the explicit teaching of vocabulary and conceptual understandings;

☐ Instructional methods are culturally and experientially biased; teaching heterogeneous groups of students requires the systematic use of instructional methods that meet the varied needs of children;

☐ There is a systematic sequence of instruction that is essential if all children in the class are to learn; this requires a systematic provision of review, overview, presentation, exercise, and summary;

☐ Teaching students how to process information requires an interactive, process approach to learning; teaching must help students understand their own thoughts and creativity through speaking and writing; and

☐ A major task of educational programs is to extend the world view of the child; this should include a view of careers, of the community, of our nation and our global community.

These principles can be applied in any number of ways—for example, as magnet schools, community schools, ungraded schools, middle schools, alternative schools, or schools within schools. While the structure of the program can be designed in a variety of ways, there must be a core understanding and implementation of the principles outlined above.

Principles for Restructuring

The implementation of any of these three approaches to restructuring is likely to produce positive benefits. There is, however, the consideration that none of the approaches is likely to result in the level of change that is desirable. If schools are truly to be restructured, they must:

☐ Be related to changes and needs in the community and society;

☐ Include the organizational restructuring of the school system itself; and

☐ Focus on the restructuring of the teaching-learning process.

A comprehensive approach to restructuring must involve each of these three areas. The goal of the restructuring is to find a "fit" between the community, the school system, and the teaching-learning process. (See the following illustration).

The Fit For Comprehensive Restructuring

Finding this fit among the three areas of restructuring is likely to ensure that the effort has dealt with three essential components for educational excellence—relevance, effectiveness, and efficiency. Knowing the community and society and responding to the forces for change begins to establish the basis for relevance and for preparing children and youth for a future society. Opening up the bureaucracy and empowering staff and students begins to offer the basis for effectiveness in providing a structure for learning. Lastly, change in the classroom provides the means for ensuring efficiency by increasing the quality and quantity of learning.

Schools may begin the restructuring process in a single area or develop comprehensive plans. Either approach has strengths and problems which must be addressed. What cannot be done is to ignore the need for change and transformation. Change must occur if schools are to achieve their contract with society to prepare children and youth for a future world.

Bruce Campbell

Bruce Campbell is a classroom teacher at Cascade Elementary School in the Marysville, Washington, School District and a designer/instructor of a summer program for "at risk" secondary students. For a number of years he has pioneered the classroom application of Howard Gardner's Theory of Multiple Intelligences, and as a result has been widely recognized as a consultant in this area. His work illustrates what can happen in the classroom when teachers integrate into their work the ideas presented in this collection.

He has been a presenter at a recent US Department of Education conference on Gardner's work, and a consultant to Indiana University, which is coordinating a gifted education program applying the Multiple Intelligences model. Numbers of schools in Indiana are currently replicating Campbell's work.

Formerly, he was director and head teacher at Horizon School, an independent elementary school in Mount Vernon, Washington. In that program he created an integrative curriculum for cross-aged classes. He has also taught in the Burlington Little School and the Sedro Wooley Schools, both in the state of Washington.

At the Evergreen State College, Antioch University, and Western Washington University he has presented seminars on both graduate and undergraduate levels. He is currently Team Captain and co-facilitator of the Western Washington Regional Tournament for "Odyssey of the Mind."

He was author and director of children's theatrical performances demonstrating current educational theory and application for two major international educational conferences. He is also the author of *Our Only Earth: The Ocean Crisis*, published by Zephyr Press; co-author (with his wife Linda MacRae Campbell and Dee Dickinson) of *Learning Works: Teaching and Learning through the Multiple Intelligences*; and a number of articles on his work have appeared in national publications.

A TEACHER'S PERSPECTIVE   Bruce Campbell, M.A.

With the relentless demands of daily teaching, educators often weary of new trends and fads in school programs. However, the information currently available from the cognitive sciences is not a slick trend designed for a "quick fix" of a faulty part in an industrial age piece of educational machinery. Instead, groundbreaking research reveals new and fundamental insights into our brain/ mind/body system and offers hope for optimizing human learning. As a classroom teacher, I have found it important to devote part of my schedule to keeping abreast of innovations in educational research, theory, and practice. So as to better meet the needs of my

185

diverse students as well as possible, I must be well informed; however, just being aware of the information emerging from the cognitive sciences is not enough. I have found that my teaching has to change in response to what I learn.

Many of the researchers and theorists highlighted in this book reveal new directions for educational practice. The work of Howard Gardner, for example, helps teachers perceive students in new ways, acknowledging children's abilities rather than disabilities. The work of Mihaly Csikszentmihalyi and Barbara Clark has implications for lesson and unit planning. Paul McClean and Marian Diamond provide glimpses into the human brain and suggest ways to optimize learning. Shirley McCune offers a rationale for changing current educational systems to fit our times.

Exposure to such new information provokes numerous questions among educators. What is a meaningful curriculum? What is the best way to present it? How should technology be incorporated? How can higher levels of thinking and problem solving be engaged? How many different kinds of intelligence can be addressed in any lesson? What about individual and cultural differences among our students? How can educators spearhead innovations in school programs and practices? These questions and others appear, at first, overwhelming. And yet instead of giving way to cynicism or resistance, educators can choose to reflect on the implications of such information. We can accept the fact that change is a constant in our professional lives and determine what is possible for each of us to apply in our classrooms or schools in our continuous efforts to improve the educational experience of our students.

Applying New Theories in a Single Classroom

In an attempt to apply some of the recent research into my own third grade classroom, I developed an instructional model primarily founded upon Howard Gardner's Theory of Multiple Intelligences. My students spend most of the day moving through seven learning centers, each devoted to one of the intelligences identified by Gardner. Curriculum is thematic and interdisciplinary. Following a lecture on the daily theme, students divide into seven groups to begin their center work. For approximately twenty minutes at each center, students learn about the day's topic through a different modality.

For example, in a recent unit on outer space, students focused on comets for one day. In the Building & Moving Center (Kinesthetic Intelligence), students made model comets with sticks, marshmallows and ribbons and then created a dance to illustrate a comet's orbit around the sun. In the Reading Center (Linguistic Intelligence), they read books about comets. In the Math & Science Center (Logical/Mathematical Intelligence), students solved story problems adding numbers for the lengths of comets' tails. In the Working Together Center (Interpersonal Intelligence), each group worked collaboratively at the computer, creating a database file on things in outer space, including comets. In the Personal Work Center (Intrapersonal Intelligence), students wrote comet poems on pieces of paper cut out in the shapes of comets. In the Art Center (Spatial Intelligence), they designed beautiful comets with glue and glitter on graph paper. The parts of their comets had to be labelled and drawn in correct proportion. In the Music Center (Musical Intelligence), each group created a rap song about comets to incorporate some of the facts they had learned. At the end of the day, poems were bound in a class book, raps were shared by each group, art work was hung on a bulletin board, and progress in other centers reviewed.

While the framework for my classroom is founded upon Gardner's Theory of Multiple Intelligences, I have also been influenced by many of the other theorists represented in this book.

To begin with, the students are directly involved in the planning process. Malcolm Knowles has clearly described the advantages of self-directed learning; and I have found that, even as young as third grade, students can capably assume partial responsibility for their education. In the above lesson, for example, the comet-shaped poem book, glitter comets, and raps were all student-suggested ideas. Students also have frequent opportunities to develop independent projects. Self-directed learning enhances intrinsic motivation which Mihaly Csikszentmihalyi suggests is crucial in education. The emphasis in my planning is to first stimulate my students' enjoyment of learning and then transmit information. Ironically, academic content is transmitted far more effectively with this focus.

David Perkins talks about the "mindware" of the human intellect. Art Costa stresses the importance of thinking skills. In an effort to incorporate their ideas, I regularly present problems to my students requiring analysis, evaluation, synthesis, and participatory decision-making. Linda Tsantis emphasizes the value and necessity of technological literacy. To engage students in useful applications of available technology, I am establishing a telecommunications project to link my classroom with another in a foreign country. Not only will this enhance reading, writing, and computing skills, it will also introduce my students to children of another culture and value system. Many observers to my classroom comment upon how confident, resourceful, and articulate my students are. Such comments underscore my gratitude to those who have inspired significant changes in my teaching.

Some Research Results in a Classroom Implementing New Theories & Research

To determine whether these instructional changes were achieving significant academic gains, I conducted an action research project in my classroom during the 1989-1990 school year. Just as implementing new educational theory has been a new experience for me, so was conducting a research project! However, with the support of educational faculty at Antioch University Seattle, I enjoyed being a reflective practitioner. Some of the results of the study are listed below:

1. The students developed increased responsibility, self-direction, and independence over the course of the year. Although no attempt was made to compare this group of students with those in other third grade classes, the self-direction and motivation of these students was apparent to many classroom visitors. The students were skilled at developing their own projects, gathering necessary resources, and making well planned, multimodal presentations.

2. Discipline problems significantly lessened. Students previously identified as behavior problems showed rapid improvement during the first six weeks of school. By mid-year, they were making important contributions to their small groups. And by year's end, they had assumed positive leadership roles, which had not formerly been evident.

3. All students developed and applied new skills. In the fall, most students described only one center as their favorite one, and the one where they felt most confident. Interestingly enough, the distribution among the seven centers was relatively even. By mid-year, most identified three to four favorite centers. By year's end, every student identified at least six centers that were favorites and where they felt skilled. Moreover, all students made multimodal presentations of independent projects, including songs, skits, visuals, poems, games, surveys, puzzles, and group participation activities.

4.   Cooperative learning skills improved in all students. Since so much of the center work was collaborative, students became highly skilled at listening, helping each other, sharing leadership, accommodating group changes, and introducing new classmates to the program. They learned not only to respect each other but also to appreciate and call upon the unique gifts and abilities of their classmates.

5.   Academic achievement improved as measured by both classroom and standardized tests. MAT scores from the previous year's students were above state and national averages in all areas. Retention was high on a classroom year end test of all areas studied during the year. Methods for recalling information were predominantly musical, visual, and kinesthetic, indicating the influence of working through the different intelligences. Students who had previously been unsuccessful in school became high achievers in new areas.

In summary, it is clear that students' learning improved. Many students stated they enjoyed school for the first time. As the school year progressed, new skills emerged. Some students discovered musical abilities, artistic, literary, mathematical and other new-found capacities. Others became skilled leaders. In addition, self-confidence and motivation increased significantly. Finally, students developed responsibility, self-reliance, and independence as they took an active role in shaping their own learning experiences.

I attribute the implementation and success of this program to my being informed about current knowledge relevant to the field of education. It is also interesting to note that the research itself had a very positive effect upon my teaching. As I evaluated incoming data, I often realized there were changes I could make to improve the quality of my program. By conducting action research, teachers have the opportunity to renew themselves professionally.

Conclusion

While the model of instruction implemented in my classroom works well for my students and myself, it is not necessarily an approach appropriate for other educators. It is the responsibility of each of us, however, to become informed of breakthroughs in human learning and teaching, to ask questions about how to apply this information and then develop methods tailored to our classrooms. Today's students are looking ahead to their futures. We will do them a disservice if we educate them in the ways of our past. The increasing diversity of our students and the global shift to the information age demand teaching methods and programs that are relevant for the soon-to-be adults of the 21st century. By keeping abreast of educational innovation, educators experience self-renewal through our own profession. We feel inspired and energized to change in ways appropriate for our times, and we model for our students the value and necessity of lifelong learning.

191

Linda MacRae Campbell

Linda MacRae Campbell is never daunted by any challenge, whether she is helping a retarded adult to learn to read, working with easily distracted young children, or motivating the interest of gifted high school students. Her greatest current interest is in teaching teachers, and her work in that area is resulting in great rewards as they apply what they have learned to teaching their own students.

She is currently the director of New Horizons for Learning and coordinator of the innovative Teacher Certification Program at Antioch University Seattle. Her continuing success as a "facilitator of change" in public schools began with her work as a restructuring consultant for the National Education Association.

As a classroom teacher, she received the Teacher of the Year awards three times. She has taught on all levels; and, as a junior and senior high school teacher, she taught language arts, French, and humanities. She was director of an award-winning drama department at Redmond High School in Washington State.

Later, as director of her own school, she received a Professional Business Woman of the Year award. She was founder and director of the Pegasus Schools, where she developed an integrative educational program for children from three to seventeen.

She is currently an adjunct professor at Seattle Pacific, Eastern Washington, and Antioch Universities, and Gifted Program Coordinator for the Burlington and Concrete Public Schools.

Her publications include *Our Only Earth: A Curriculum for Global Problem-Solving* (a series of six books integrating science, social studies, and language arts). Her *No Time to Waste* and *We All Live Downstream* are environmental manuals commissioned by Greenpeace. She is also co-editor with Dee Dickinson of New Horizons for Learning's journal, *On the Beam,* and co-author of *Learning Works: Teaching and Learning Through the Multiple Intelligences.*

FACILITATING CHANGE
IN OUR SCHOOLS

Linda MacRae-Campbell, M.A.

At present, numerous schools across the country have accepted the challenge of updating and upgrading their services. However, as administrators and faculties forge ahead to rethink their educational mission, organizational structure, academic program, teaching methods, personnel roles, or community relationships, their renewal efforts often falter because schools lack effective action plans. Many involved in efforts to change are unaware of guidelines for the successful initiation and implementation of an innovation. By working with a game plan, even if it requires frequent modification, schools can avoid unnecessary wheel spinning and prevent excessive time loss to process issues. Determining where a school is going and how it will arrive can make educational reform less stressful, more predictable and manageable, and most importantly, more successful for all involved.

While the restructuring experience will vary from school to school, renewal efforts at any site can be well strategized and coordinated. To manage the change process efficiently, some guidelines follow that highlight essential aspects and issues of educational reform. It should be noted that the nature of restructuring is non-linear and that the following guidelines will not necessarily unfold in a predictable sequence:

ORGANIZING RESTRUCTURING: GUIDELINES FOR CHANGE PROJECTS

Guideline 1: Identify a new mission or a need for reform within the school.

Restructuring can begin only with the initiation of honest dialogue at a school. This is often difficult to achieve since many teachers and administrators are resistant to any perceived change effort, are hesitant to speak truthfully about problems, or else they opt to maintain a collegial, "let's not rock the boat" school climate. One interesting observation some educational reformers have made is that when teachers are asked to assess their school, many believe it is above average. Faculties assume that serious problems exist elsewhere but not at their own site. Those who promote school renewal will necessarily and frequently have to engage individuals, small groups, and full faculty meetings in repeated school appraisal and restructuring conversations. Dialogue of all kinds, both informal and formal, both low key and hard hitting, must be risked before a school will determine it has reason to change.

Many restructuring efforts begin by targeting a high profile need or concern within a school. Serious issues such as dropout rates, lack of parental involvement, or too many curricular add-ons can be highlighted. Supporting "evidence" of the extent of the problem should also be shared, and will frequently catalyze individuals to action and insure widespread support. An example of targeting a high-profile need to intiate restructuring was recently evident at an urban high school of 1600 students. Some staff members had, understandably, become concerned with the failure statistics of its ninth grade students. At the end of the first semester, 450 ninth graders generated over 500 class failures. While many faculty members placed blame on outside factors for the dismal academic performance, several maintained that action should be taken to prevent such failure from recurring.

A major restructuring effort was launched by a committee of approximately 12 members, including teachers, administrators, parents, and a school counselor. After a year of research, heated debate, discussion, and grant writing, a significant alteration of the school's program was proposed. An entire wing of the school building was dedicated to house the incoming ninth grade students for four hours each day.

Five "schools within schools" were created for the ninth graders; teachers and counselors were reassigned to accommodate approximately 90 students each; an interdisciplinary curriculum was developed; new instructional methods were pursued; and extensive parental outreach was initiated. Plans are currently under way to spread the "school within a school" concept throughout the entire high school program. Ultimately, by beginning with one high-profile issue, the essentials of schooling at this high school were radically redesigned to better meet the needs of its students.

Another approach to instigating significant change is to write or update an educational misson statement. Many schools have not specified their philosophy, goals, and values; this oversight results in a lack of purpose and vision for such sites. Without a cohesive mission statement, schools exist merely to adhere to the rules and regulations imposed by outside agencies; they are thus unprepared for self-determination. A mission statement clarifies a school's identity and underscores its distinct individuality.

Writing such a mission statement requires extensive preliminary dialogue among all members of the school community: teachers, administrators, students, parents, community members, and classified staff. Once clearly articulated, however, all academic and extracurricular offerings, curricula, teaching methods and most importantly, staffing, should reflect the school's stated purpose in operation. To achieve such internal integrity usually requires significant restructuring efforts.

One middle school, besieged with the acute inner-city problems of gang violence, drug abuse, low standardized achievement scores, and poor staff morale, determined that significant improvement must occur to maintain staff and enhance the academic program. Weary of focusing on what was wrong, a group met with the principal to discuss how they might revitalize the school. It was evident that the teachers and administrator wanted to be enthusiastic about what they were doing; they wanted a new burst of life and energy to fill them personally and to spark the students with a love for learning. The group determined that the way to move their middle school forward was to create a new mission, one which would provide a schoolwide impetus for change.

From discussions with the school community, the new mission quickly emerged: the school would become the state's first arts-based school. Later, a full mission statement was drafted which specified, in part, that the arts would be used not only as specific disciplines taught by art specialists, but as an integral part of classroom instruction in all subjects, as the source of schoolwide projects and activities and as one avenue to increase interaction with parents and local community members. Extensive revision of the school's program was undertaken, as was the retraining of staff members. The few teachers who did not agree with the the new mission statement were encouraged to transfer elsewhere in the district to insure integrity in the new program and its practice.

Educational renewal is often a conflict-ridden process. As they begin honest and earnest dialogue about their schools, faculties commonly find it necessary to seek training in conflict resolution skills, problem-solving, and decision-making approaches. Assuming the role of change agent requires the honing of a variety of new skills in order to complete the tasks at hand successfully.

Guideline 2: Seek support for educational change.

Support for change efforts can come in two forms: information that provides reformers with a solid knowledge base to work from, advocacy from those inside and outside the school. During the last twenty or so years, an explosion of research from the cognitive sciences has revealed ways to optimize learning and teaching. It is indefensible not to implement what is currently known about improving human learning potential. Many of the researchers represented in this book serve as guides into new educational terrain.

As schools endeavor to upgrade their programs, they can look to the current knowledge base for both inspiration and support.

Providing rationales for change efforts founded upon solid research helps persuade many naysayers. Educational innovators who are well informed of the breakthroughs in the cognitve sciences are intellectually and often politically empowered as they begin to influence school philosophy, policy, and practice.

When a change effort is initiated, strong advocates for the innovation from within and outside of the school should be identified and their support actively sought. By offering a variety of ways to participate, more individuals can contribute to the restructuring effort. It is unrealistic, however, to expect that any innovation will be greeted with consensus and also highly unlikely that a majority of those involved will embrace the innovation. Fortunately, consensus and majority favor are not necessary to initiate change. Many significant restructuring projects have gotten under way with the support of only 15 to 20 % of a school's population. Some change projects have begun with as few as two supporters.

As an example, at one high school of approximately 50 teachers, two teachers decided to team their first and second period classes. Since this arrangement had little or no impact on the other teachers, scant attention was paid at first to the teamed and interdisciplinary approach; however, the student response was enthusiastic and vociferous. They wanted more similar courses, and, a year later, their requests were met. What began as a two-person project quickly escalated into a schoolwide instructional approach.

Guideline 3: Create and communicate a model of the change effort.

To reduce the rampant cynicism among most school staffs about educational improvement, restructuring endeavors should be well organized and coordinated. A written and/or visual model of the change effort can be developed and posted, including timelines, activities, task force members, and their responsibilities. One middle school decided to track its accomplishments on a monthly basis. In the faculty lounge, a large monthly calendar was made and posted on the faculty bulletin board. Meeting dates, tasks, and accomplishments were logged, as were sneak previews into the projects ahead. Such a simple visual tracking device served to keep the faculty informed, and meanwhile conveyed the important message that things were being accomplished.

It's often wise to specify short-term, intermediate, and long-term goals with renewal endeavors. Beginning with small projects that gain visibility and success within the first three to four months can increase confidence as well as demonstrate that achievements are being made. For far-reaching restructuring plans, many reformers suggest a minimum of three to five years for developing, implementing, and institutionalizing new models.

Ways to measure the effects and results of the innovation can also be undertaken. School personnel will find it valuable to evaluate their efforts and then use such data to determine their next steps. As research is conducted, it can be shared with other reformers and restructuring sites, thus making important contributions to the expanding knowledge base of school renewal. One highly innovative approach to conducting and sharing research is evident in the National Education Association and IBM partnership that has linked teachers across the United States electronically, enabling them to telecommunicate their research and build upon each each other's experience.

Guideline 4: Secure needed resources.

A variety of resources must be secured to implement any kind of educational innovation successfully. Both human and material resources will be required, including consultations, training programs, financial support, and curriculum materials. Extensive and on-going staff development must become a regular feature of school life so that educators can keep abreast of the knowledge base and continually broaden their range of educational tools.

Usually, the most important resource, and the one in least supply, is additional *time* for those involved in restructuring. While confronted with the relentless demands of teaching, school personnel must have time to reflect on what must change as well as time to implement the changes. To accommodate this need, many schools have creatively altered their daily schedules to provide meeting time for staff members. Some sites begin five minutes earlier each day to "buy" two half days of release time every month. One school provides a full release day each week per teacher. This is accomplished by having faculty work longer days four days out of five, resulting in one full day of preparation or staff development time. Other approaches have included coordinating teachers' schedules to create team or group planning time; adding paid work days beyond the school calendar; and hiring substitutes to release teachers to conduct restructuring projects.

Guideline 5: Acknowledge the emotional reaction to change.

School renewal is rarely an objective, rational process. Change agents should anticipate their own emotional reactions to change, as well as strong reactions from others. Some researchers have studied the affective dimension of restructuring with fascinating findings about the emotional response to change.

In the 1979 *Annual Handbook for Group Facilitators*, University Associates, Don Kelly and Darryl Connor have identified an emotional cycle of change, which includes five stages:

1. **Uninformed optimism** is the honeymoon phase of the project and provides the energy and enthusiasm to begin the restructuring effort.

2. **Informed pessimism** ensues when unexpected problems are encountered, the resistance of others rears up, and morale drops. This is a dangerous stage of the emotional cycle, and many change efforts are abandoned during this phase. For those projects that continue, the three remaining three stages include:

3. **Hopeful realism** when it is evident that some efforts will succeed in spite of the obstacles;

4. **Informed optimism** which emerges when confidence is restored as things move ahead, and

5. **A sense of rewarding completion** which is experienced by those involved in the change effort as they see concrete results of their work.

Another emotional phenomenon encountered in restructuring is the "Implementation Dip" identified by Michael Fullan, author of *The Meaning of Educational Change*. When people agree to implement a new procedure or policy, a decline in performance or work quality is commonly experienced during their initial attempts. This can be so humiliating and frustrating that feelings of awkwardness and guilt often emerge. It is important, however, to note that the decline in skills is only temporary. Once the dip has been reached, behavior usually reorganizes itself at a higher level than before.

Anyone attempting to initiate change within a school must also realize that some others will openly, verbally, resist the change. Occasionally, the resistance takes the form of professional or personal attacks. Emotional fortitude, a sense of humor, and a personal support system are usually necessary to sustain the commitment of any change agent. Since the emotional rollercoaster ride of educational innovation appears inevitable, being forewarned of the ups and downs can, at least intellectually, make the ride more bearable.

Guideline 6: Anticipate restructuring problems and identify problem-solving skills.

Taking a proactive approach to predictable restructuring problems serves to streamline and accelerate change efforts. In his research of schools embracing change, Matthew Miles, professor at the University of Massachusetts, has identified their common renewal problems. These include, in order of importance: attitude and emotional issues; process factors such as lack of coordination, planning, or communication; and lack of resources. Other predictable problems are unanticipated crises, competing demands, limiting physical environments and perceived low or minimal control among those involved in the change effort.

Change facilitators may want to plan how to handle such problems before they arise. Matthew Miles has also identified a variety of problem-solving strategies, and he asserts that active problem-solving methods are extremely important if a project is to be successful. Passive avoidance, procrastination, doing things the usual way, and shuffling people from task to task are weak strategies. Effective problem solving approaches include vision-building and sharing, monitoring progress and revising plans accordingly, securing outside assistance, re-staffing if necessary, team-building, increasing resource control, and redesigning the school organization.

Since each change effort is undoubtedly fraught with problems, it is crucial to use myriad coping skills. Sensing what is appropriate for any situation is an important intuitive skill to develop. At times, deliberate postponement may be the best approach; however, empowering school staff, establishing new roles and groups, and monitoring and adjusting efforts often reduce restructuring problems.

Guideline 7: Share the leadership.

For widespread change to take hold, it is necessary to share control of the project and to work collaboratively with others. Securing both input and follow-through from diverse groups such as teachers, administrators, classified staff, students, parents, consultants, and school board and community members will effectively broaden the support base.

To distribute leadership equitably, one high school developed a new governing body. This group, called the Representative Council, includes teachers, administrators, counselors, classified staff, students, and parents. Membership requirements consist of a personal commitment to attend the bi-monthly meetings for the entire school year. The R.C. oversees two main components of the high school: ongoing daily affairs and the school's philosophy. Thus, in a highly democratic manner, it assumes responsibility for establishing the mission and conducting the operation of the high school on a daily basis.

For successful restructuring it is also necessary to develop effective communication channels. Information can be shared at weekly meetings, through newsletters, bulletin items, phone trees, or other means. One elementary school placed a journal on a podium in the staff lounge. Anyone was free to write individual or schoolwide messages about the renewal efforts. The resulting avid interest in the journal was not anticipated. It provided a powerful link and voice in the restructuring effort. Another elementary school, wanting to enlist broad community support for its continual progress, ungraded school program, created a high quality newsletter published monthly. The photographs, articles, and interviews explore successes and challenges of the innovative model while maintaining one important communication channel with community members.

Guideline 8: Anchor the innovation as quickly as possible to classroom practice.

The ultimate goal of all restructuring projects is to enhance the learning of children and the teaching of teachers in schools suitable for our time. Change efforts must necessarily be linked to classroom practice and the sooner the better. Skepticism about improvement efforts is reduced when teachers are asked to expand their instructional and assessment repertoires. When change facilitators address the nitty gritty of school life and of teaching and learning, educational innovations appear relevant and important.

For new classroom practices to be implemented, both support and pressure are required. Encouragement and technical assistance should be offered freely as deadlines are met, new teaching approaches adopted, and results achieved. Also important are the rewards and recognition offered for innovators at each school site.

Recently, one elementary school made a commitment to change instructional strategies in each classroom. All staff members received training in learning styles theory. Each teacher then identified ways to apply learning styles concepts to his teaching. The students were informed of their teachers' efforts. Banners were then hung in each classroom stating, "Each student in this classroom has the right to learn through his/her strengths at least some of the time." The banner exerts gentle pressure for teachers to remain on track with their commitment and guarantees students that their learning styles will be actively engaged. The banners have become a source of pride to teachers who eagerly point them out to classroom visitors as they explain the schoolwide effort to "teach to reach" each student.

Guideline 9: Embed the renewal effort and process into organizational practice.

Once implemented, measured, and refined, the restructuring effort becomes part of organizational life. When it has become embedded in many aspects of school life, including its philosophy, budget, policies, and practices, increasing numbers of personnel will make use of the change. Even when significant results are achieved and celebrated, however, renewal efforts are not complete. Restructuring is a process that must become a regular feature of school life, enabling continual initiation, implementation, and institutionalization of change within each school.

The world, and the mass of information at our disposal, are being transformed rapidly, and schools must create processes to keep abreast of and implement new approaches to education, teaching, technology and human development. When school personnel perceive change as synonymous with learning, then ongoing restructuring will be the norm, and schools will evolve into learning organizations.

Educational innovation can be understood, managed, and valued as positive results are achieved. Schools can derive satisfaction from taking charge of their destinies and leading the restructuring movement forward, rather than being pushed into it. There is also great satisfaction in helping our schools better meet the needs of children they serve. These children are waiting for us to act.

LOOKING FORWARD Dee Dickinson

Robert Sternberg describes intelligence as "not only the ability to learn and apply what has been learned in order to adapt to the environment, but the ability to modify the environment, or seek out and create new environments." That is creating one's own future and that is what education should equip all students to do.

But that is not all. Human ingenuity and technology have solved complex problems and created breakthroughs in every field; however, without the ability to anticipate the consequences of our actions, other, more complex problems may result. We live in a world in which the thinking and decisions of human beings have resulted in stockpiling nuclear weapons, destroying or polluting the environment, causing social catastrophes, and doing physical violence to others.

Many of the people responsible have been awarded high degrees in education and have accumulated a great deal of knowledge and experience. What is really important, however, is the quality of that education and the ability to apply that knowledge and to learn from experience.

In today's world we can no longer ignore the critical responsibilities of all educators to instill in the young the values and ethics that will equip them to make not only wise but humane and moral decisions. Children must be given opportunities to develop such higher order thinking skills as altruism, empathy, and human understanding—to develop self-esteem and the capability to love— to be able to plan ahead and foresee the consequences of their decisions and actions.

The responsibility for instilling or teaching these greatest of all human capacities cannot lie in the home alone at a time when many families are fragmented, do not have or take the time, or may not value the importance of such principles. Although parents must certainly be given opportunities to learn how to create positive environments and teach these values, none the less every social institution must now also share in the responsibility if the planet is to survive.

And so we have no choice except to intensify the painful dialogue about educational change that reflects a new world view, beginning with a new understanding about the unlimited potential of the individual human brain and mind. What we experience, what and how we learn, what we think, and how we behave all have an effect on the mental, physical, emotional, and spiritual capacities that we will make use of—and, it is to be hoped, continue to develop—for the rest of our lives.

Parents, caregivers, teachers, and we ourselves all carry a responsibility to make the most of our possibilities. In order to do so, we must continue to learn all we can from cognitive and educational research. We must learn from studies in human development that offer strategies we can use to enrich our lives and that will also affect the lives of those with whom we live and work and play.

Each of the foregoing writers has a specific insight to offer, but it is the complementary power of all their ideas that is helping to bring about positive change in every educational setting. These ideas are making a difference in the learning that takes place in homes among both parents and children; in schools, universities, and adult education programs among both teachers and students; in workplaces among both trainers and employees; and in centers for the elderly among both caregivers and senior citizens. And these ideas are also being recognized by policy makers and school administrators in their planning and budgeting.

Following is an attempt to integrate some of the key concepts presented in the foregoing articles:

☐ Belief systems are changing about what is possible in human development at every age and ability level. It is essential to acknowledge and implement what is already known, much of which is not new. Stories of successful teachers abound, from the ancient times of Socrates and the great leaders of all religions, to great teachers such as Maria Montessori and Annie Sullivan, and to the many fine, often unsung, teachers of our own times. Research abounds, yet often lies unread and ignored. Successful projects that have led to unexpected success with students perceived as being less than able have been documented and shelved. Many new theories, including Dr. Reuven Feuerstein's Theory of Structural

Cognitive Modifiability, are transforming the world of education and are laying the foundation for the fullest possible human development of each individual. It is not news that it is possible to find a way for everyone to learn, yet too often we fail to act on that truth.

☐ With the increasing diversity in the population of every country in the world, individual differences are being recognized as strengths through which to learn. Often culturally-based, these include perceptual differences, differences in personality and learning styles, and differences in the kinds of intelligence described by Drs. Gardner, Perkins, and Sternberg. It has been recognized as well, by such researchers as Drs. Diamond and Feuerstein, that cognitive levels are affected not only by heredity but opportunity.

☐ The emotional context of learning, as noted by many of the authors, is now well recognized as having a critical effect on either facilitating or inhibiting learning and human development. The studies of both Drs. Diamond and MacLean point to the importance of creating positive, nurturing, and stimulating environments, and offering much opportunity for interaction. Motivational factors are also at the heart of the "deep learning" described by Dr. Entwistle.

☐ Basic to any successful teaching method that involves and develops higher order thinking skills is the Mediated Learning Experience, as developed by Dr. Feuerstein. Various forms of this method involve interaction between the students and teacher and are the opposite of systems in which the student is the passive recipient of facts and information.

☐ The polarities that have resulted from pendulum swings throughout educational history are now beginning to come together. Many schools and classrooms are recognizing the importance of integrating mind, body, and spirit. And many schools are integrating different subjects through such methods as thematic curriculum and team teaching.

☐ At a time when school administrators, parents, and business people are demanding that teachers cover more content and equip students with greater proficiency in the basic skills, it is crucial to recognize that high content and high process must go hand in hand.

It is essential to identify the most important knowledge and skills that students need in order to survive and thrive in today's and tomorrow's world. Then the most appropriate, efficient teaching and learning strategies must be employed to help all students to be successful in learning what they need to know.

As Colin Rose points out, these strategies can be integrated into a variety of effective methods that all teachers and all students can learn easily. These methods lay the foundation for successful educational systems, successful students, and successful adults.

☐ The use of technology is becoming increasingly widespread and is now an essential skill for students of every age. In addition to accelerating learning, it offers opportunities to explore and expand intelligence, quick positive feed-back, access to unlimited sources of information, international communication, distance learning, and the possibility of in-servicing large numbers of teachers simultaneously.

☐ The arts are being recognized as languages that speak to cultural and individual differences, that increase the repertoire of skills for communication and understanding, that present opportunities to exercise higher order thinking skills, and offer avenues for self-expression and enhancement of self-esteem.

The schools in which they are being taught not only as separate subjects but are integrated throughout the curriculum, and which devote a significant part of each day to the arts, are among the highest achieving schools academically. This is true not only in the United States but in other countries as well, including Hungary, the Netherlands, and Japan—the three nations producing the highest student achievement in science today.

☐ New methods of assessment are being implemented as it is recognized that when tests focus on memorization and recall, they do not encourage teachers to emphasize such important results of learning as practical application, problem-solving, analysis and synthesis, and metaphorical thinking. These new tests include the assessment of a wider range of intelligence as described by Drs. Gardner and Sternberg, and the assessment of student learning through essays, portfolios of student work, projects, and other means of observing the student's ability to comprehend and apply what has been learned.

☐ New methods of giving recognition to successful teachers and schools are being implemented, as there is recognition

212

that intrinsic motivation is usually more powerful than extrinsic rewards, aside from adequate compensation, of course. Often successful teachers and schools have gone unnoticed or have been demeaned and put down by their colleagues in dysfunctional systems. Some schools have actually lost funding as students have overcome their learning disabilities. Appreciative recognition in ways that reinforce and help to replicate success include offering mini-grants for special projects, leadership roles, positions as in-house consultants, or opportunities to be teacher trainers.

☐ Restructuring is a word that is on every educator's lips, but it means different things to different people. As described by Dr. McCune and others, it is being applied to reformulating curriculum, methods of teaching, use of time and facilities, reallocation of staffing, and the exploration of new roles for teachers and new ways of preparing them. Restructuring is responding to a new world view that demands that students be equipped to think internationally, to cope with rapid change, and to develop all their capacities as fully as possible.

☐ Collaboration has become a major theme in the school reform movement, as site-based management becomes the norm. As Dr. McCune points out, it is clearly essential, in order to meet student needs that are not being met through any other source, for teachers and school administrators, social-service, health, welfare, and other community agencies, parent groups, and businesses to work together in this most important of all social enterprises.

The skills of working collaboratively are most easily developed early in life. It is often difficult for adults to learn

213

interpersonal skills if they have not had an opportunity to work cooperatively as students. For this reason, as well as the fact that for many students cooperative learning is faster, longer-lasting, and a more positive experience than either individualized or competitive models of education, this strategy has become standard practice in a growing number of educational settings.

☐ An international, multicultural context for education is now recognized as essential, as all parts of the world can be immediately connected electronically and as the speed of air travel increases. Many of the strategies previously described are being used to meet the needs of culturally diverse student populations in every setting. The pluralistic world view referred to by Drs. Costa and Hilliard is not being learned from most textbooks, but rather from personal experiences in the classroom, reinforced by real or electronic pen pals and either real or electronic, often interactive, field-trips to sites in other countries.

☐ Community learning centers, as foreseen by Dr. Knowles long ago, are multiplying in a variety of forms throughout the United States and in other countries as well. In the United States, one form was instituted with the "lighted schoolhouse" model in Flint, Michigan thirty years ago; another variation was developed as community colleges were created.

Today many schools are running nearly "around the clock," providing schooling during the day for children and also offering programs for day-care and early childhood, adult literacy, and senior citizens, who also provide effective models for lifelong learning. Many of these centers offer social, health, and welfare services on-site. After school, such centers offer adult education and worker training and retraining programs.

The traditional closed system of education, in which standardization has been the norm, and in which the same material has often been taught in the same way year after year, must now give way to a truly open system and all that implies.

As Malcolm Knowles suggests, "We must become able not only to transform our institutions in response to changing situations and requirements; we must invent and develop institutions that are 'learning systems,' that is to say, systems capable of bringing about their own continuing transformation."

As information doubles yearly in many fields—in the sciences often in a matter of months—many textbooks are obsolete before they are printed. Teachers must now rely upon more current sources of information not only through new publications, but through the vast array of databases. The diversity of students necessitates a variety of teaching methods and technology, constantly expanding. Teachers who were isolated from the rest of the world in their own classrooms are now able to collaborate with other local teachers and resource personnel, as well as having access to electronic support systems of other teachers and resource personnel elsewhere in their own country or others.

Educational systems, unlike other large businesses or professions, have rarely had research and development centers to guide their work. There is now an unequivocal need to create a research and development system to support the groundswell of change happening in thousands of classrooms. These are often the sources of the most exciting educational innovations, born out of desperate need to find a better way to help all students to learn.

215

A prototype of an interactive, electronic research and development system was developed by the Mastery in Learning Project described by Dr. McClure, linking NEA schools to the Boyer, Sizer, and Goodlad networks. Another has been developed under the leadership of Jay McTigh at the state Department of Education in Maryland, linking all schools electronically to a multi-media database to which teachers have both access and input.

Just a step away is the creation of a global, interactive, multi-media database to make the most current information available to all teachers anywhere in the world. This database could indeed facilitate the development of the long-needed research and development system for education wherever it takes place.

The technology is now available to link networks and databases not only as sources of information on well-researched educational strategies and programs, but on incipient models as well. Program planners and teachers could have immediate access to a support system of the most current information, could ask questions, share their own work, and receive quick feedback from others working in similar areas.

Such a system will surely become the driving force in educational change, built on the current grassroots revolution occurring today in classrooms throughout the world. The human race can no longer afford the individual egotism, institutionalism, and national territoriality that have prevented valuable information on education and human development from being shared. Self- and system-imposed limitations will dissipate as educational systems come into their own as creators of the future. Dr. Sternberg's definition of intelligence may then apply to such systems that will lead humanity forward to an era of the "global learning society" in which everyone will have the freedom to learn. Nothing less would be worthy of the most important natural resource on earth—the human mind.

Dee Dickinson

Dee Dickinson is president and founder of New Horizons for Learning, an international education network based in Seattle, Washington. She is also co-editor of the network's quarterly journal, *On the Beam*. She served as a member of the White House Task Force on Innovative Learning, and is currently Educational Advisory Board chairperson of the National Learning Foundation.

Dee has taught on all levels from pre-school through university and has produced several series for educational television. Formerly, she was director of the Seattle Creative Activities Center and vice president of the International Association for Accelerative Learning, based at the University of Rio de Janeiro. She is an internationally recognized speaker and consultant to educational and corporate groups, and has produced six international conferences.

She is author of *New Horizons for Learning: Creating an Educational Network* and co-author, with Linda MacRae Campbell and Bruce Campbell, of *LearningWorks: Teaching and Learning Through the Multiple Intelligences*. Her report, *Positive Trends in Learning: Meeting the Needs of a Rapidly Changing World*, was commissioned and published by the IBM Corporation in 1991.

Selected Bibliography

Botkin, James; Elmandjra, Mahdi; and Mircea, Malitza. *No Limits to Learning.* NY: Permagon Press, 1979.

Campbell, Linda MacRae. *No Time to Waste* and *We All Live Downstream.* NY: Greenpeace, 1990.

—— *Our Only Earth: A Curriculum for Global Problem-Solving.* Tucson, AZ: Zephyr Press, 1990.

Clark, Barbara. *Growing Up Gifted.* Columbus, OH: Merrill, 1979. *Optimizing Learning.* NY: Charles Merrill, 1988.

Costa, Arthur. *Supervision for Intelligent Teaching.* Sacramento, CA: Midwest Publications, 1989.

—— *Developing Minds* (ed.) Alexandria, VA: ASCD, 1985.

Costa, Arthur and Lowery, L.F. *Techniques for Teaching Thinking* Pacific Grove, CA: ASCD, 1989.

Csikszentmihalyi, Mihaly and Csikszentmihalyi, Isabella. *Optimal Experience.* Cambridge: Harvard University Press, 1988. *Flow, The Psychology of Optimal Experience.* NY: Harper and Row, 1990.

Diamond, Marian Cleeves. *Enriching Heredity.* NY: Macmillan, 1988.

Entwistle, N. J. "Motivational Factors in Students' Approaches to Learning." In R.R. Schmeck (ed.) *Learning Strategies and Learning Styles.* NY: Plenum 1988.

—— *The Experience of Learning* (ed.) Edinburgh: Scottish Academic Press, 1989.

—— *The Handbook of Educational Ideas and Practices* (ed.) London: Routledge (1990).

Feuerstein, Reuven; Rand, Yaacov; and Hoffman, Mildred. *The Dynamic Assessment of Retarded Performers: The Learning Potential Assessment Device.* Baltimore: University Park Press,1979.

—— *Instrumental Enrichment: An Intervention Program for Cognitive Modifiability.* Baltimore: University Park Press, 1980.

Feuerstein, Reuven; Rand, Yaacov; and Rynders, John. *Don't Accept Me As I Am.* NY: Plenum Press, 1988.

Fowler, Charles. *Can We Rescue the Arts for America's Children?* NY: American Council for the Arts, 1988.

Gardner, Howard. *Art, Mind and Brain.* NY: Basic Books, 1982.
    Frames of Mind. NY: Basic Books, 1983.
—— *The Mind's New Science.* NY: Basic Books, 1985.
—— *To Open Minds.* NY: Basic Books, 1989.
Healy, Jane. *Your Child's Growing Mind.* NY: Doubleday, 1987.
—— *Endangered Minds: Why Our Children Don't Think.* NY: Simon
    and Schuster, 1990.
Houston, Jean. *Lifeforce.* NY: Dell, 1982.
—— *The Possible Human.* Los Angeles, CA: J.P. Tarcher, 1982.
—— *Mind Games.* NY: Marlboro, 1990.
Knowles, Malcolm. *The Adult Learner: A Neglected Species.* Houston,
    TX: Gulf, 1984.
—— *Andragogy in Action.* San Francisco, CA: Jossey-Bass, 1984.
—— *The Making of An Adult Educator.* San Francisco, CA: Jossey-
    Bass, 1989.
Machado, Luis Alberto. *The Right to Be Intelligent.* NY: Permagon
    Press, 1980.
MacLean, Paul D. *The Triune Brain in Evolution.* NY: Plenum, 1990.
McCune, Shirley. *Guide to Strategic Planning for Educators.* Alexandria,
    VA: ASCD, 1986.
Perkins, David. *The Mind's Best Work: A New Psychology of Creative
    Thinking.* Cambridge, MA: Harvard University Press, 1983.
—— *Knowledge As Design.* Hillsdale, New Jersey: Erlbaum, 1986.
Perkins, David; Nickerson, Raymond; and Smith, Edward. *Teaching
    Thinking.* Hillsdale, New Jersey: Erlbaum, 1985.
Rose, Colin. *Accelerated Learning.* NY: Dell, 1985
Sternberg, Robert. *Beyond I.Q.* NY: Cambridge University Press,
    1985.
—— *Applied Intelligence.* NY: Harcourt Brace Jovanovich, 1986.
—— *The Triarchic Mind: A New Theory of Intelligence* NY: Viking
    Press, 1988.
—— *Wisdom: Its Nature, Origins, and Development* (ed.) NY:
    Cambridge University Press, 1990.
Taylor, Anne, and Vlastos, George. *School Zone: Learning Environments
    for Children.* Corrales, NM: School Zone, Inc. 1983.

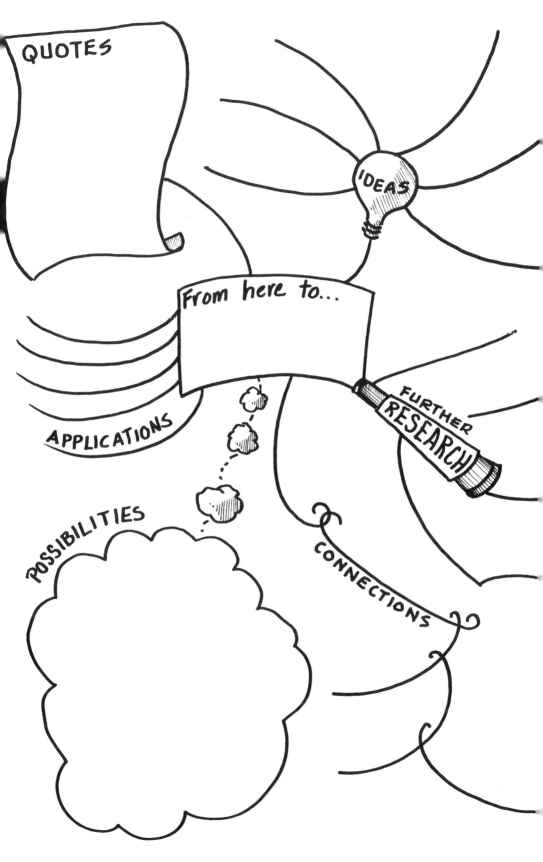

A CONTRIBUTION TO CHANGE

Creating the Future is one in a series of publications which we hope will make a practical contribution to the challenges that face education and training. These include:-

- A teacher handbook, entitled *Learning Works*, demonstrating how the concept of Multiple Intelligences can be successfully implemented in the classroom.

- A series of *Learn to Learn* programs ranging from immediate post natal advice, through pre-school learning, to a student and adult course on learning skills.

- A *Training and Development Program* which ensures that trainees of diverse learning styles are accommodated within a single training class.

- A series entitled *Yes, You Can!* . . . This includes courses on drawing, mathematics and thinking skills.

- A series of home study *Foreign Language Courses* that accommodate a full range of learning preferences.

Please contact any of the addresses below:

Accelerated Learning Systems Ltd., 50 Aylesbury Road, Aston Clinton, Aylesbury, Bucks. HP22 5AH. UK Tel: (0296) 631177

or

Accelerated Learning Systems Inc., 3028 Emerson Ave. South, Suite 1, Minneapolis, MN 55408. US Tel: (612) 827 4856

New Horizons for Learning also publishes a quarterly newsletter called *On the Beam*. It is designed to communicate significant developments in educational theory and practice.

4649 Sunnyside N.,
Seattle, WA. 98103 US
Tel: (206) 547 7936